COWLES FOUNDATION
For Research in Economics at Yale University

MONOGRAPH 17

THEORY OF VALUE
An Axiomatic Analysis
Of Economic Equilibrium

GERARD DEBREU

NEW HAVEN AND LONDON, YALE UNIVERSITY PRESS

Printed in the United States of America by
LithoCrafters, Inc.,
Chelsea, Michigan.

Published in Great Britain, Europe, Africa, and Asia
(except Japan) by Yale University Press, Ltd., London.
Distributed in Australia and New Zealand by Book &
Film Services, Artarmon, N.S.W., Australia; in Japan by
Harper & Row, Publishers, Tokyo Office.

TO ALFRED COWLES

CONTENTS

1. MATHEMATICS 1

  1. Introduction. – 2. Sets. – 3. Functions and Correspondences. – 4. Preorderings. – 5. Real Numbers. –
6. Limits in R^m. – 7. Continuous Functions. – 8. Continuous Correspondences. – 9. Vectors in R^m. –
10. Fixed Points. – Notes.

2. COMMODITIES AND PRICES 28

  1. Introduction. – 2. Dates and Locations. – 3. Goods.
– 4. Services. – 5. Commodities. – 6. Prices. – 7. Interest, Discount, and Exchange. – 8. Theory and
Interpretations. – Notes.

3. PRODUCERS 37

  1. Introduction. – 2. Productions and Production
Sets. – 3. Assumptions on Production Sets. – 4. Profit
Maximization. – 5. Price Variations. – Notes.

4. CONSUMERS 50

  1. Introduction. – 2. Consumptions and Consumption
Sets. – 3. Assumptions on Consumption Sets. – 4. Preferences. – 5. Insatiability Assumption on Preferences.
– 6. Continuity Assumption on Preferences. – 7. Convexity Assumptions on Preferences. – 8. Wealth Con-

straint. – 9. Preference Satisfaction. – 10. Price-Wealth Variations. – Notes.

5. EQUILIBRIUM   74

    1. Introduction. – 2. Resources. – 3. Economies. – 4. Attainable States. – 5. Private Ownership Economies. – 6. Market Equilibrium. – 7. Equilibrium. – Notes.

6. OPTIMUM   90

    1. Introduction. – 2. Optimum and Equilibrium Relative to a Price System. – 3. An Equilibrium Relative to a Price System Is an Optimum. – 4. An Optimum Is an Equilibrium Relative to a Price System. – Notes.

7. UNCERTAINTY   98

    1. Introduction. – 2. Events. – 3. Commodities and Prices. – 4. Producers. – 5. Consumers. – 6. Equilibrium. – 7. Optimum. – Notes.

REFERENCES   103

INDEX   109

    Symbols. – Names and Terms.

PREFACE

The two central problems of the theory that this monograph presents are (1) the explanation of the prices of commodities resulting from the interaction of the agents of a private ownership economy through markets, (2) the explanation of the role of prices in an optimal state of an economy. The analysis is therefore organized around the concept of a price system or, more generally, of a value function defined on the commodity space.

The first solutions of the two preceding problems were achieved by L. Walras [1] and V. Pareto [1], [2], [3], [4] respectively, but neither the masters of the school of Lausanne nor their disciples for several decades gave a very rigorous account of their ideas. For example, the knot of the first problem was thought to be cut by the bold assertion that a system of equations whose number equals that of its unknowns can be solved. Only in 1935–36 did A. Wald [1], [2], [3] publish the first rigorous analysis of the problem of equilibrium. A little earlier J. von Neumann [1], [2] had begun to develop, in different contexts, a mathematical tool which was eventually to play an essential role in that area under the definitive form as a fixed point theorem it received from S. Kakutani [1]. The value of that tool for economics was demonstrated in 1950 by J. Nash's [1] proof that every finite n-person game has an equilibrium point (a concept whose origin can be traced to A. Cournot [1], Chapter 7). As for the second problem, the first rigorous study, using convex sets properties, of the equivalence be-

tween an optimum and an equilibrium relative to a price system was
done by T. C. Koopmans [1] in the context of linear activity analysis
of productive efficiency. The research of the last decade reported in
this volume started from these contributions. But it is hardly necessary to add that many other currents of ideas have, directly or in-
directly, influenced the substance or the form of that research. Outstanding among these influences has been the work of J. von Neumann
and O. Morgenstern [1] which freed mathematical economics from its
traditions of differential calculus and compromises with logic.

The theory of value is treated here with the standards of rigor of
the contemporary formalist school of mathematics. The effort toward
rigor substitutes correct reasonings and results for incorrect ones, but
it offers other rewards too. It usually leads to a deeper understanding
of the problems to which it is applied, and this has not failed to happen
in the present case. It may also lead to a radical change of mathematical tools. In the area under discussion it has been essentially a
change from the calculus to convexity and topological properties, a
transformation which has resulted in notable gains in the generality
and in the simplicity of the theory.

Allegiance to rigor dictates the axiomatic form of the analysis where
the theory, in the strict sense, is logically entirely disconnected from
its interpretations. In order to bring out fully this disconnectedness,
all the definitions, all the hypotheses, and the main results of the
theory, in the strict sense, are distinguished by italics; moreover, the
transition from the informal discussion of interpretations to the formal
construction of the theory is often marked by one of the expressions:
"in the language of the theory," "for the sake of the theory," "formally." Such a dichotomy reveals all the assumptions and the logical
structure of the analysis. It also makes possible immediate extensions
of that analysis without modification of the theory by simple reinter-
pretations of concepts; this is repeatedly illustrated below, most
strikingly perhaps by Chapter 7 on uncertainty.

To keep the cost associated with such an axiomatization at a minimum, the theory is consistently set forth in the simplest possible
mathematical framework even when immediate generalizations, some
of which will be mentioned in notes, are available. In addition, the
small amount of mathematics necessary for a full understanding of
the text (but not of all the notes) of Chapters 2 to 7 is given in the
first chapter in a virtually self-contained fashion. In another respect
the reading of this monograph will be facilitated by the excellent intro-
ductions to its problems provided by T. C. Koopmans' [2] first essay

and by R. Dorfman, P. A. Samuelson, and R. M. Solow's [1] Chapters 13, 14.

Before concluding, must one remark that the contents of this volume—which have been taught at the University of Chicago and at Yale University since the spring of 1953, and presented as a Doctor of Science thesis at the University of Paris in June 1956—do not try to exhaust the theory of value? Several important questions left unanswered are emphasized below. One may stress here the certainty assumption made, at the level of interpretations, throughout the analysis of Chapters 2 to 6, according to which every producer knows his future production possibilities and every consumer knows his future consumption possibilities (and his future resources if resources are privately owned—otherwise only the future *total* resources, need be known). This strong assumption is weakened, albeit insufficiently, in the last chapter.

The Cowles Foundation has provided an uncommonly favorable environment for the research from which this monograph evolved, and I wish to express my gratitude to Alfred Cowles, its founder, and to Tjalling C. Koopmans and Jacob Marschak for the constant interest they have taken in my work. I have an exceptional debt to Kenneth J. Arrow, for several of the main ideas of this volume have been advanced either independently (K. J. Arrow [1], G. Debreu [1]), or jointly (K. J. Arrow and G. Debreu [1]) by him and by me. Tjalling C. Koopmans, Lionel W. McKenzie, Jacob Marschak, Roy Radner, and Robert M. Solow have read the whole manuscript or extensive parts of it, and I owe many searching comments to them. My concern for the theory of the school of Lausanne arose when I first met it in the treatise of Maurice Allais [1] and, a little later, in the book of François Divisia [1]. I also thank them, Georges Darmois, Wassily Leontief, Pierre Massé, René Roy, and James Tobin for having greatly helped to create the conditions which made this investigation possible. Finally I gratefully acknowledge the financial support of the Office of Naval Research and the Social Science Research Council in the writing of this text, of the Centre National de la Recherche Scientifique, the Rockefeller Foundation, and the RAND Corporation in the preliminary work that led to it.

CHAPTER 1

MATHEMATICS

1.1. Introduction

This chapter presents *all* the mathematical concepts and results which will be used later (in notes, however, additional concepts and results will be freely used). Its reading requires, in principle, *no* knowledge of mathematics.

The exposition starts from the concept of a set of elements and gradually introduces, by means of definitions, concepts of increasing complexity. Simultaneously results concerning those concepts are stated. Sections 1.2, 1.3, and 1.4 stay at a high level of generality; they deal respectively with sets, functions and correspondences, and preorderings. Section 1.5 is a crucial step in the exposition; it introduces (real) numbers. To prepare for their definition it is necessary to introduce earlier the concepts of a binary operation (in 1.3.j) and of a least upper bound (in 1.4.g). From the set R of (real) numbers, one builds up the Euclidean space of m dimensions, R^m. Section 1.6 centers on the concept of a convergent sequence of points of R^m. Sections 1.7 and 1.8 are respectively devoted to the concepts of continuity of functions and of correspondences. Section 1.9 is built on the definitions of the sum of two elements of R^m and of the product of an element of R^m by a (real) number; it considers R^m as a vector space. Section 1.10 studies the concept of fixed point of a correspondence.

The method of exposition chosen parallels that of contemporary mathematics; one of its aims is to show mathematical concepts in their proper light. This is of invaluable help in the formulation and the solution of economic problems.

It was stated that the reading of this chapter requires no knowledge of mathematics. This is, admittedly, true only "in principle." It certainly requires an ability to think abstractly, which is usually developed through the practice of mathematics, and an ability to assimilate in a short time

1

a certain number of new concepts the motivation for which may not always be clear at first. On the other hand, the expert will notice that the logical foundations of set theory and even an elementary knowledge of the integers are taken for granted.

The concepts and results which will be presented form the strict minimum necessary for a complete understanding of later chapters. For example, theorem (6) of 1.6.n (every subset of R^m contains a dense countable set) is necessary for the proof of existence of a utility function in Chapter 4, section 6; theorem (16) of 1.9.x (the Minkowski bounding hyperplane theorem for convex subsets of R^m) is, in essence, the central result on economic optimum which is proved in Chapter 6, section 4; theorem (2) of 1.10.d (the Kakutani fixed point theorem for correspondences from a convex subset of R^m to itself) is, in essence, the central result on economic equilibrium which is proved in Chapter 5, sections 6 and 7.

Furthermore those concepts and results are almost all among the most basic of mathematics, and their usefulness goes far beyond the applications which are made of them below.

Yet the reader may lack the time to read this entire chapter and the proofs of the economic theorems for which it prepares. The text of the following chapters has therefore been presented in such a way that the concepts and results stand out clearly and their meaning can be grasped with still less mathematical preparation.

In this chapter, proofs of assertions are not given. In many cases the reader could reconstruct them; it might then be a valuable exercise for him to do so; hints will sometimes be provided. When this reconstruction offers difficulties the locution "One can prove . . ." or some explicit warning is used. Small-type passages contain examples and heuristic comments. They are irrelevant for the logical development of the text proper and could be omitted entirely; it is therefore permissible, in them, to draw upon an intuitive knowledge of the physical world, and to use undefined simple mathematical terms like distance, curve, rectangle, . . .

1.2. Sets

a. A *set* S of *elements* is also a *collection* of *elements*; sometimes one says a *class* of *elements*.

EXAMPLES: (1) The set A of actions available to a certain social agent and among which he has to choose. (2) The set N of *positive integers*, or whole numbers, $\{1, 2, 3, \cdots\}$ (braces will denote sets).

b. The sets which constitute the universe of discourse must always be explicitly listed at the outset.

EXAMPLE: A social system may be described as composed of a certain number *m* of agents. Any one of these agents may be indicated by a positive integer *i*, one of the positive integers 1, 2, $\cdots$, *m*. For any one of them, say the *i*th one, a set A_i of available actions is given. The universe of discourse consists of the *m* sets $A_1, \cdots, A_m$.

c. $x \in S$ expresses that *x* denotes a certain element of *S*; it is read: *x belongs* to *S*, or *x* is an element of *S*, or *x* is in *S*, or *S owns x*.

EXAMPLE: $a_i \in A_i$ indicates that a_i is an action available to the *i*th agent.

d. If *x*, *y* denote elements of *S*, then $x = y$ (*x equals y*) expresses that they denote the same element, and $x \neq y$ (*x different* from *y*) expresses that they denote different elements.

e. Let $\mathscr{P}$ be a *property* which any element *x* of *S* has or does not have. $\{x \in S \mid x \text{ has property } \mathscr{P}\}$ denotes the set of all the elements of *S* which have property $\mathscr{P}$; it may be read: the set of *x* in *S* such that *x* has property $\mathscr{P}$.

EXAMPLE: If *A* is the set of actions available to an agent and *a'* is an element of *A*, the set of those available actions which that agent considers more desirable than *a'* is $\{a \in A \mid a \text{ is preferred to } a'\}$.

f. A set *X* of elements of *S* is called a *subset* of *S*; this is denoted by $X \subset S$ (*X contained* in *S*). The notation $X \subset S$ does not exclude the possibility that *X* is equal to *S*.

EXAMPLE to emphasize the last point: $N \subset N$ (the set of positive integers).

g. Careful distinction must be made between the *element* *x* of *S* and the *subset* $\{x\}$ of *S* having the only element *x*.

EXAMPLE: The assertion $x \in X$ is equivalent to the assertion $\{x\} \subset X$.

h. A property $\mathscr{P}$ defines a subset of *S*, namely the set of elements of *S* having that property. When no element of *S* has the property $\mathscr{P}$, one says that $\mathscr{P}$ defines the *empty* subset of *S* denoted $\emptyset$. This convention is necessary if a property is *always* to define a subset of *S*.

EXAMPLE: In the example of 1.2.e, $\{a \in A \mid a \text{ is preferred to } a'\}$ is always a subset of *A*. If *a'* happens to be the most desirable action in *A*, then the above set is the empty subset of *A*.

i. If *X* is a subset of *S*, and *x* an element of *S*, then $x \notin X$ expresses that *x* is *not* an element of *X* (*x* does not belong to *X*). The elements of *S* which do not belong to *X* form a set called the *complement of X in S* and denoted $\mathbf{C}_S X$. When there can be no ambiguity about S one says the *complement of X*, and one writes $\mathbf{C} X$.

j. Let X and Y be two subsets of S. One defines $X \cup Y$, the *union* of X and Y, as the set of elements of S belonging to X or to Y (or to both). $X \cap Y$, the *intersection* of X and Y, is the set of elements of S belonging to both X and Y. If X and Y have no element in common, i.e., if $X \cap Y = \emptyset$, they are said to be *disjoint*.

EXAMPLES can easily be constructed by drawing two (overlapping or non-overlapping) regions X, Y in a plane S.

k. More generally, let $\mathfrak{X}$ be a set of subsets of S. The *union* of these subsets, $\bigcup_{X \in \mathfrak{X}} X$, is the set of elements of S which belong to at least one X in $\mathfrak{X}$. Their *intersection*, $\bigcap_{X \in \mathfrak{X}} X$, is the set of elements of S which belong to all the X in $\mathfrak{X}$.

l. A collection $\mathfrak{X}$ of subsets of S forms a *partition* of S if they are *pairwise disjoint* (i.e., if any two different subsets belonging to $\mathfrak{X}$ are disjoint) and if their union is S. That is, if each element of S belongs to one and only one of the subsets in $\mathfrak{X}$. A partition of a set corresponds to the familiar idea of a classification of its elements.

m. Consider two sets S and T; the set of *pairs* (x, y) where $x \in S$ and $y \in T$, is called their *product* $S \times T$. The order in which x, y and S, T are written in (x, y) and $S \times T$ is essential.

EXAMPLE: Let S be the lower horizontal edge of a rectangle drawn in a plane and T its left vertical edge. If x is a point of S, y a point of T, the pair (x, y) may be visualized as the intersection point of the vertical straight line through x and the horizontal straight line through y. The product $S \times T$ is then visualized as the region covered by the rectangle.

n. More generally, consider m sets $S_1, \cdots, S_i, \cdots, S_m$. The set of *m-tuples* $(x_1, \cdots, x_i, \cdots, x_m)$, where $x_i \in S_i$ for every $i (= 1, \cdots, m)$ is the *product* $S_1 \times \cdots \times S_i \times \cdots \times S_m$, also denoted $\prod_{i=1}^{m} S_i$. The order in which the x_i and the S_i are written is again essential. The m-tuple $(x_1, \cdots, x_i, \cdots, x_m)$ is denoted by (x_i), and x_i is called the *i*th *coordinate* (or the *i*th *component*) of (x_i).

EXAMPLE: Consider a social system consisting of m agents. The ith agent must choose an action a_i in a given set A_i of actions available to him. When each agent has made his choice, the outcome of the social activity is determined. Thus social activity is characterized by an m-tuple (a_i), an element of $\prod_{i=1}^{m} A_i$.

1.3. Functions and Correspondences

a. Let S and T be two sets; if with each element $x \in S$ is associated one and only one element $y \in T$, a *function f* from S to T is defined. f is also called a *transformation* of S into T. x is the *variable*, y is the *image* of x by f, or the *transform* of x by f, or the *value* of f at x, and one writes $y = f(x)$ (read y equals f of x), or $x \rightarrow f(x)$.

EXAMPLE: Let A be the set of actions available to a certain agent. If the choice of a in A determines the amount of money (a positive integral number of cents) this agent receives, a function from A to N is defined.

b. Consider in $S \times T$ the set of elements (x, y) for which $y = f(x)$. This subset of $S \times T$ is called the *graph* of the function f.

EXAMPLE: In the example of 1.2.m, the graph of a function f from S to T is visualized as a set of points of the rectangle such that the vertical through an arbitrary point x of S intersects it at exactly one point.

c. Let X be a subset of S; take the image $y = f(x)$ of each $x \in X$. The set of the images so obtained is a subset of T called the *image* of X and denoted $f(X)$. If $f(S)$ consists of one element of T, in other words, if all the elements of S have the same image in T, the function f is said to be *constant*. If $f(S) = T$, in other words, if each element of T is the image of some element of S, f is said to be a function from S *onto* T.

d. Conversely, let Y be a subset of T; the set of $x \in S$ which have their images in Y is a subset of S called the *inverse image* of Y and denoted $\overset{-1}{f}(Y)$.

EXAMPLE: If a curve is taken as graph of f in the example of 1.3.b, a proper choice of X, Y gives illustrations of the concepts of 1.3.c and 1.3.d.

It is easy to prove that:

(1)   *If f is a function from a set S to a set T, and if $\mathfrak{Y}$ is a collection of subsets of T, then $\overset{-1}{f}(\bigcap_{Y \in \mathfrak{Y}} Y) = \bigcap_{Y \in \mathfrak{Y}} \overset{-1}{f}(Y)$.*

e. A $y \in T$ may be the image of several, or of one, or of no element of S. When for each $y \in T$ the set $\overset{-1}{f}(y)$ consists of exactly one element, in other words, when each $y \in T$ is associated with one and only one element of S, f is said to establish a *one-to-one correspondence* between S and T. This concept will be further discussed in 1.3.n.

f. Let f be a function from a set F to a set T, and let G be a set containing F. A function g from G to T is said to be an *extension of f to G* if one has $f(x) = g(x)$ for every x in F.

5

g. Consider n sets $S_1, \cdots, S_j, \cdots, S_n$ and their product $\prod_j S_j$. The function which associates with the generic element (x_j) of $\prod_j S_j$ its ith coordinate x_i in S_i is called the ith *projection* (or the *projection on S_i*). The image of an element (resp. of a set) by a projection function is called the *projection* of that element (resp. of that set).

h. If with each element x in a given set S is associated a *non-empty* subset Y of a given set T, a function φ from S to the set of subsets of T is defined. It is sometimes preferable to consider φ as a *correspondence* from S to T. One writes $Y = \varphi(x)$.

EXAMPLES: (1) Let f be a function from a set S onto a set T; for every $y \in T$, $\overset{-1}{f}(y)$ is a non-empty subset of S, hence $\overset{-1}{f}$ is a correspondence from T to S. (2) Let A be the set of *a priori* available actions of a social agent. Suppose that his environment is completely specified by an element e of a set E. His environment restricts his freedom of action, i.e., the element e determines the subset of A to which his choice is actually restricted. A correspondence from E to A is thus introduced.

i. The *graph* of the correspondence φ is a subset of $S \times T$, namely $\{(x, y) \in S \times T \mid y \in \varphi(x)\}$.

EXAMPLE: Consider the case of the rectangle already used to illustrate the graph of a function in 1.3.b; the graph of a correspondence from S to T is visualized as a set of points of the rectangle: the intersection of this set with a vertical through an arbitrary point x of S is a non-empty set (the projection of which on T is $\varphi(x)$). See also fig. 2.a and fig. 2.b of 1.8.

j. A *binary operation* $\top$ on a set S associates with each pair (x, y) of elements of S (the order of which is essential) a unique element z of S. One writes $z = x \top y$. Thus a binary operation on S is nothing else than a function from $S \times S$ to S.

EXAMPLES: (1) The addition of two positive integers is a binary operation $+$ on N. (2) So is the multiplication $\cdot$ of two positive integers. (3) Given two positive integers x, y, the expression x^y denotes the product of y positive integers equal to x; thus a binary operation $\wedge$ on N can be defined by $x \wedge y = x^y$.

k. A binary operation $\top$ on S is said to be *associative* if for all x, y, z in S one has $(x \top y) \top z = x \top (y \top z)$. It is said to be *commutative* if for all x, y in S one has $x \top y = y \top x$.

EXAMPLES: (1) Both $+$ and $\cdot$ on N are associative and commutative. (2) $\wedge$ on N is neither associative nor commutative.

l. Consider two binary operations $\perp$ and $\top$ defined on S. The first is said to be *distributive* with respect to the second if for all x, y, z in S one has $z \perp (x \top y) = (z \perp x) \top (z \perp y)$.

EXAMPLES: (1) On N, $\cdot$ is distributive with respect to $+$. (2) But $+$ is not distributive with respect to $\cdot$.

m. A *sequence* $(x^1, x^2, x^3, \cdots, x^q, \cdots)$ of elements of a set S is an intuitive concept. Precisely, it is defined as a function from N to S. It will be denoted by (x^q).

n. Intuitively, a set S is *countable* if it has at most as many elements as N. In a precise fashion, a set S is defined as countable if it can be put in one-to-one correspondence with a subset of N. When the countable set S is not empty one can always choose the corresponding subset of N so that it owns 1, and so that, whenever it owns two positive integers, it owns every positive integer between them. The image of $x \in S$ in the correspondence is then called the *rank* of x. Thus a set is countable if and only if all its elements can be ranked, no two different elements having the same rank. One can prove that

(2)   *The product of m countable sets is countable.*

EXAMPLES: (1) $N \times N$ is countable. (2) However, one can prove that the set of subsets of N is *not* countable.

1.4. PREORDERINGS

a. Let $\mathscr{R}$ be a *binary relation* in which any *two* elements x, y of S (the order of which is essential) stand or do not stand. If they do, one writes $x \mathscr{R} y$.

EXAMPLES: (1) Let $\mathfrak{S}$ be the set of subsets of a set S. The relation $\mathscr{R}$ on $\mathfrak{S}$ might be "is contained in," then $X \mathscr{R} Y$ would be equivalent to $X \subset Y$; (2) or the relation $\mathscr{R}$ might be "does not intersect," then $X \mathscr{R} Y$ would be equivalent to $X \cap Y = \emptyset$. (3) Let A be the set of actions available to an agent; the relation $\mathscr{R}$ might be "is not preferred to." (4) Consider the relation "is not a successor of" on N and denote it by $\leq$.

b. The last relation corresponds to the natural ordering of the elements of N. To define with full generality an ordering relation on a set, one preserves certain properties of $\leq$ on N. In a precise manner, a binary relation $\mathscr{R}$ on S which satisfies

(1) $x \mathscr{R} x$ for every $x \in S$ (*reflexivity*),
(2)   "$x \mathscr{R} y$ and $y \mathscr{R} z$" implies "$x \mathscr{R} z$" (*transitivity*)

is called a *preordering* (often also a *quasi-ordering*). When, in addition, "$x \mathscr{R} y$ and $y \mathscr{R} x$" implies "$x = y$," the relation is called an *ordering*. Often the symbol $\precsim$ will be used (in place of $\mathscr{R}$) to denote a preordering. By definition, $y \succsim x$ means $x \precsim y$.

EXAMPLES: In the examples of 1.4.a, the first and the fourth relation are preorderings (in fact, they are orderings), the second is not. The third will always be assumed below to be a preordering; "a^1 is not preferred to a^2" will be denoted $a^1 \precsim a^2$; this relation is not necessarily an ordering.

c. "$x \precsim y$ and $y \precsim x$" is written "$x \sim y$." "$x \precsim y$ and not $y \precsim x$" is written "$x \prec y$" (or "$y \succ x$").

EXAMPLES: In the last example, $a^1 \sim a^2$ is read "a^1 is indifferent to a^2," and $a^1 \prec a^2$ is read "a^1 is less desired than a^2" or "a^2 is preferred to a^1."

d. Two elements x, y of a preordered set may not be comparable (as the example of the preordering $\subset$ emphasizes). When one necessarily has $x \precsim y$ or $y \precsim x$ (or both), the preordering is called *complete* (to emphasize that a certain preordering is not necessarily complete, one calls it *partial*). Then $x \precsim y$ is the negation of $x \succ y$.

EXAMPLE: The preordering "is not preferred to" on the set of actions available to an agent will always be assumed below to be complete.

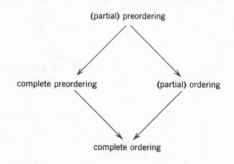

Fig. 1

e. Figure 1 summarizes the different types of preorderings. An arrow indicates decreasing generality.

f. Let S be a *partially preordered* set. When $y \in S$ and there is no $x \in S$ such that $x \succ y$ (resp. $x \prec y$), y is called a *maximal* (resp. *minimal*) element of S. When $y \in S$ and for all $x \in S$ one has $x \precsim y$ (resp. $x \succsim y$), y is called a *greatest* (resp. *least*) element of S. A greatest (resp. least) element of S is clearly a maximal (resp. minimal) element of S. When the preordering is complete the converse is also true and the distinction disappears. When the preordering is an ordering there is at most one greatest element and at most one least element.

EXAMPLES: (1) Consider the set N partially ordered by the relation "is a divisor of," and let S be $\{1, 2, 3, 4, 5\}$. S has three maximal elements, 3, 4, 5, no greatest element, one minimal element, 1, and one least element, 1. (2) Consider a set A of actions completely preordered by the relation "is not preferred to." If a is an action to which none is preferred, a is a greatest element of A (which need not be unique: there may be other greatest elements, all indifferent to a).

g. Let S be a preordered set, and consider a subset X of S. An element $y \in S$ such that for all $x \in X$ one has $x \precsim y$ (resp. $x \succsim y$) is called an *upper bound* of X (resp. a *lower bound* of X). Consider the set Y of the upper bounds of X; the set Y has the property: "$y \in Y$ and $y' \succsim y$" implies "$y' \in Y$." A least element of Y is a *least upper bound* of X. If X has a greatest element y, y is clearly a least upper bound. The concept of *greatest lower bound* of X is similarly introduced.

h. In the next section, the requirement will be put on a certain ordered set that every non-empty subset which has an upper bound has a least upper bound.

i. Let S be a preordered set. A subset I of S is an *interval* if "$x \in I$, $y \in I$, and $x \precsim z \precsim y$" implies "$z \in I$." Let a, b be two elements of S such that $a \precsim b$; particular cases of intervals are:

$$[a, b] = \{x \in S \mid a \precsim x \precsim b\}, \qquad]a, b[= \{x \in S \mid a \prec x \prec b\},$$

$$[a, b[= \{x \in S \mid a \precsim x \prec b\}, \qquad]a, b] = \{x \in S \mid a \prec x \precsim b\},$$

$$[a, \rightarrow[= \{x \in S \mid a \precsim x\}, \qquad]\leftarrow, b] = \{x \in S \mid x \precsim b\}.$$

j. Denote by $S_1, \cdots, S_i, \cdots, S_m$ m preordered sets, by $\precsim$ the preordering on S_i, by x_i a generic element of S_i. A preordering $\precsim$ is defined on the product $S = \prod_{i=1}^{m} S_i$ by $(x_i) \precsim (x_i')$ if $x_i \precsim x_i'$ for every $i (= 1, \cdots, m)$. According to the general notation of 1.4.c, $(x_i) \prec (x_i')$ means that (α) for all i, $x_i \precsim x_i'$ and (β) *not* for all i, $x_i' \precsim x_i$, i.e., (β) for at least one i, $x_i \prec x_i'$. The notation $(x_i) \prec\prec (x_i')$ will express that, for all i, $x_i \prec x_i'$. With the exception of trivial cases, the preordering $\precsim$ on S cannot be complete.

EXAMPLE: See 1.9.z.

k. Let S and T be two preordered sets, and denote by $\underset{S}{\precsim}$ (resp. $\underset{T}{\precsim}$) the preordering on S (resp. on T). A function f from S to T is said to be *increasing* (or to be a *representation* of S in T) if "$x \underset{S}{\precsim} x'$" implies "$f(x) \underset{T}{\precsim} f(x')$" and "$x \underset{S}{\prec} x'$" implies "$f(x) \underset{T}{\prec} f(x')$."

9

1.5. REAL NUMBERS

a. The set R of (*finite, real*) *numbers* is *defined* as a set of elements having the following properties (all familiar, perhaps with the exception of the last one).

b. There are on R two associative and commutative binary operations (*addition* $+$, *and multiplication* $\cdot$). *There is an element, 0, which, if added to any element x, gives x. Any element x has a negative, i.e., an element which, if added to x, gives 0. There is an element, 1, which if multiplied by any element x, gives x. Any element x different from 0 has an inverse, i.e., an element which, if multiplied by x, gives 1. Multiplication is distributive with respect to addition. 0 is different from 1.*

c. There is on R a complete ordering denoted $\leq$. If z is any element and $x \leq y$, then $x + z \leq y + z$. If $0 \leq x$ and $0 \leq y$, then $0 \leq x \cdot y$.

d. Finally, every non-empty subset X of R which has an upper bound has a least upper bound.

e. A few definitions and further (*derived*) properties of R will now be added. $x + y$ is the *sum* of x and y, $x \cdot y$ is their *product*. If $x_1, \cdots, x_j, \cdots, x_n$ are n elements of R, their sum is denoted $\sum_{j=1}^{n} x_j$. The product of n elements equal to x is denoted x^n and called the nth *power* of x. 0 (resp. 1) is the *only* element having the property which defines 0 (resp. 1). Any $x \in R$ has a *unique* negative denoted $-x$. One writes $x - y$ for $x + (-y)$. The corresponding binary operation is called *subtraction*, and the result *difference*. Any $x \in R$ different from 0 has a *unique* inverse denoted $1/x$. One writes x/y for $x \cdot 1/y$. The corresponding binary operation is called *division*, and the result *quotient*. For any $x \in R$ one has $0 \cdot x = 0$, and $(-1) \cdot x = -x$. The multiplication dot will now always be dropped.

f. $x \leq y$ (resp. $x < y$) is read *x less than or equal to y* (resp. *x less than y*). $x \leq 0$ (resp. $x < 0$) is read *x non-positive* (resp. *x negative*). The expressions are transposed in an obvious way if the *inequality* sign is inverted. One has $0 < 1$.

g. A greatest (resp. least) element of a subset X of R, if it exists, is unique (1.4.f); it is called the *maximum* (resp. *minimum*) of X and denoted Max X (resp. Min X). One defines the *absolute value* $|x|$ of a number x by $|x| = \text{Max} \{x, -x\}$, and the *sign* of a number $x \neq 0$ by sign $x = x/|x|$. One has $|x + y| \leq |x| + |y|$.

h. A least upper bound of a subset X of R, if it exists, is unique (1.4.f); it is called the *supremum* of X and denoted Sup X. Every non-empty subset X of R which has a lower bound has a unique greatest lower bound called the *infimum* of X and denoted Inf X.

The simplest EXAMPLE is provided by the non-empty interval $I = [a, b[$. It has no maximum, its supremum is b. Its minimum, and therefore (1.4.g) its infimum, is a. See also example (2) of 1.5.o.

i. The infimum (resp. supremum) of a real interval is also called its *origin* (resp. *extremity*). The *length* of an interval with origin a and extremity b is $b - a$.

j. By repeated addition of 1 to 0, and repeated subtraction of 1 from 0, one obtains the set J of *integers* (non-negative and non-positive) as a subset of R.

k. A real number of the form p/q, where $p \in J$, $q \in J$, and $q \neq 0$, is called a *rational* number. The set of rationals, a subset of R, is denoted by Q.

(1) *The set Q is countable*

(use (2) of 1.3.n to prove that J, then Q is countable) and satisfies all the axioms in the definition of R with the exception of the last one. (For example, one can prove that the set $\{x \in Q \mid x^2 < 2\}$ has no least upper bound in Q, using the fact that there is no rational y satisfying $y^2 = 2$.)

l. One can prove that the set R is *not* countable. One can also prove that

(2) *if x, y belong to R and satisfy $x < y$, there is a rational r such that $x < r < y$.*

m. Given a number $x \geq 0$ and a positive integer n, one can prove that there is a unique $y \geq 0$ such that $y^n = x$. One calls y the nth *root* of x, and one writes $y = x^{1/n}$.

n. Consider a sequence (x^q) of numbers. Intuitively, one says that (x^q) *converges* (or *tends*) *to* the number x^0 if x^q is as close to x^0 as one wishes provided that q is large enough. In a precise fashion, (x^q) converges to x^0 if, for any number $\varepsilon > 0$, there is an integer q' (depending on ε) such that $q > q'$ implies $|x^q - x^0| < \varepsilon$. One writes $x^q \to x^0$.

o. A sequence which tends to a number is called *convergent*. It is clear that "$x^q \to x^0$ and $x^q \to y^0$" implies "$x^0 = y^0$"; thus a convergent sequence tends to a unique number called its *limit*.

EXAMPLES: (1) The sequence $((-1)^q/q)$ tends to 0 since, given $\varepsilon > 0$, making $1/q < \varepsilon$ is equivalent to making $q > 1/\varepsilon$. (2) Note that if X is the set $\{1/1, 1/2, \cdots, 1/q, \cdots\}$, then X has no minimum and Inf $X = 0$. (3) The sequences $((-1)^q)$ and (q) are not convergent.

p. The elements of R are also called *points*. The set R may be visualized as follows. On a horizontal straight line, two different points are chosen; they will represent 0 and 1, 1 being to the right of 0. An element x of R is then represented by a point of the straight line at distance $|x|$ from 0, to the right (resp. left) of 0 if x is positive (resp. negative).

q. The letters N, J, Q, R have throughout this volume the meanings introduced respectively in 1.2.a, 1.5.j, 1.5.k, 1.5.a.

1.6. LIMITS IN R^m

a. The set R^m is the product of m sets equal to R, i.e., $R \times \cdots \times R \times \cdots \times R$. According to the general definitions of 1.2.n, an element, or *point*, x of R^m is an m-tuple of real numbers $x = (x_i) = (x_1, \cdots, x_i, \cdots, x_m)$. The ith number in the m-tuple is the ith coordinate of x.

b. The set R^2 may be visualized as follows. Draw in a plane a horizontal and a vertical straight line. The first (resp. second) set R in $R \times R$ will be represented by the horizontal (resp. vertical) line by choosing 0 at the intersection point, and 1 arbitrarily to the right of 0 (resp. above 0). Then an element (x, y) of R^2 is represented by the intersection point of the vertical through x and the horizontal through y.

c. To visualize R^3, consider, in ordinary space, the west-east, the south-north, and the vertical straight line through a point 0. They will represent respectively the first, the second, and the third set in $R \times R \times R$. An element (x, y, z) of R^3 is represented by the intersection point of the vertical south-north plane through x, the vertical west-east plane through y, and the horizontal plane through z.

d. R^m is called the *m-dimensional Euclidean space*. Let I be a subset of the set of the first m positive integers $\{1, 2, \cdots, m\}$. The set $\{x \in R^m \mid x_i = 0 \text{ if } i \notin I\}$ is called a *coordinate subspace* of R^m. Its *dimension* is the number of elements of I. The point 0, all of whose coordinates are equal to 0, is the *origin* of R^m.

e. Consider a sequence (x^q) of points of R^m. One says that (x^q) *converges* (or *tends*) *to* a point x^0 of R^m if, for all coordinates $(i = 1, \cdots, m)$, one has $x_i^q \to x_i^0$. One writes $x^q \to x^0$.

f. As in the case of numbers (1.5.o), a sequence which tends to a point is called *convergent*; the unique point to which a convergent sequence tends is called its *limit*.

g. Let X be a subset of R^m; a point $x \in R^m$ is *adherent to X* if there is a sequence of points of X tending to x. One can also say, in a looser manner, that x is adherent to X if there are points of X arbitrarily close to x. Any point x of X is adherent to X; it suffices to take the sequence whose points are all equal to x.

h. The set of the points of R^m adherent to X is called the *adherence* (often also the *closure*) of X, and denoted $\bar{X}$. According to the last remark of 1.6.g:

(1) $X \subset \bar{X}$.

It is also clear that:

(2) $X \subset Y$ implies $\bar{X} \subset \bar{Y}$.

EXAMPLES: (1) Let k be a positive real number, and consider, in R^2, the square (with perimeter excluded) $X = \{x \in R^2 \mid |x_i| < k \text{ for } i = 1, 2\}$; then $\bar{X} = \{x \in R^2 \mid |x_i| \leqq k \text{ for } i = 1, 2\}$. (2) Using (2) of 1.5.1, one obtains $\bar{Q} = R$: the adherence of the set of rationals is the set of reals.

i. A subset X of R^m is *closed* if it owns its adherent points. This may be expressed as $\bar{X} \subset X$. Thus, because of (1), X is closed if and only if it is equal to its adherence. One may also say that a set is closed if and only if every point at zero distance from the set belongs to the set; this requirement will often be imposed below.

EXAMPLES: (1) In the examples of 1.6.h, X, the subset of R^2, and Q, the subset of R, are not closed; $\bar{X}$ is closed. (2) The subset of R, $\{0, 1, 1/2, 1/3, \cdots, 1/q, \cdots\}$, is closed.

j. One can prove:

(3)   *If X is a subset of R^m, its adherence $\bar{X}$ is closed.*

That is, $\bar{X} = \bar{\bar{X}}$. Since every closed set containing X clearly contains $\bar{X}$, the adherence of X can be characterized as the smallest closed set containing X.

k. It is easy to prove that:

(4)   *If $\mathfrak{X}$ is a set of closed subsets of R^m, their intersection, $\bigcap_{X \in \mathfrak{X}} X$, is a closed subset of R^m.*

It is a little more difficult to prove that:

(5)   *If $X_1, \cdots, X_j, \cdots, X_n$ are n closed subsets of R^m, their union, $\bigcup_{j=1}^{n} X_j$, is a closed subset of R^m.*

l. Let S be a subset of R^m; for a subset X of S, one defines the *adherence of X in S* as the set of points of S adherent to X. Similarly X is said to be *closed in S* if it owns the points of S adherent to X.

EXAMPLES: (1) Let k be a positive real number, and take $S = \{x \in R^2 \mid |x_i| < k \text{ for } i = 1, 2\}$, $X = \{x \in S \mid x_1 \geqq 0\}$. From a sketch it will be clear that the set X is closed in S but *not* closed in R^2. (2) Note also that any subset T of R^m is closed in T.

m. Substituting "the adherence in S" for "the adherence," "closed in S" for "closed," and S for R^m everywhere in (1) to (5), one obtains new theorems with the same proofs.

n. One can prove:

(6)   *Every subset S of R^m contains a countable set X such that $S \subset \bar{X}$.*

In other words, an arbitrary (therefore perhaps non-countable) subset S of R^m contains a countable set X which is *dense* in S, i.e., such that for any point x of S there are points of X arbitrarily close to x.

EXAMPLE: Let S be R^m itself. From $\bar{Q} = R$ (example (2) of 1.6.h) follows $\overline{Q^m} = R^m$. Thus Q^m, the product of m sets equal to Q, i.e., the set of points of R^m whose coordinates are all rational, is dense in R^m. Moreover Q^m is countable (apply (2) of 1.3.n to the m countable sets Q).

o. Let X be a subset of R^m; a point $x \in R^m$ is *interior to* X if it is not adherent to the complement of X. This means, intuitively, that x is completely surrounded by points of X. Any point x of R^m interior to X clearly belongs to X. The *interior* of X is the set of points interior to X, viz., $\mathbf{C}(\overline{\mathbf{C}X})$.

EXAMPLES: (1) Let k be a positive real number, and consider, in R^2, the closed square $X = \{x \in R^2 \mid |x_i| \leq k$ for $i = 1, 2\}$; its interior is $\{x \in R^2 \mid |x_i| < k$ for $i = 1, 2\}$. (2) The set Q^2 and the straight line $Y = \{y \in R^2 \mid y_2 = 0\}$ in R^2 have empty interiors.

As in the case of 1.6.1, if X is a subset of S (a subset of R^m), a point $x \in S$ is said to be *interior to* X *in* S if it is not adherent to $\mathbf{C}_S X$, the complement of X *in* S.

EXAMPLE: (3) Consider, in R^2, the straight line $S = \{z \in R^2 \mid z_1 = 0\}$, and its subset $Z = \{z \in R^2 \mid z_1 = 0, 0 \leq z_2 \leq 1\}$. The interior of Z in S is $\{z \in R^2 \mid z_1 = 0, 0 < z_2 < 1\}$; its interior in R^2 is empty.

p. Let X be a subset of R^m; a point in R^m is a *boundary point* of X if it is adherent to both X and its complement $\mathbf{C}X$. The *boundary* of X is the set of its boundary points, viz., $\bar{X} \cap \overline{\mathbf{C}X}$.

EXAMPLES: In the last group of examples, the boundary of the closed square X is its perimeter, that of Q^2 is R^2, that of Y is Y.

q. Let X be a subset of R^m; the *exterior* of X is the complement of its adherence, viz., $\mathbf{C}\bar{X}$. It is easy to prove that the interior, the boundary, and the exterior of X form a partition of R^m or, what is equivalent, that the interior and the boundary of X form a partition of the adherence of X. The last remark shows that the set X is closed if and only if it contains its boundary.

r. Let x be an element of R^m; its *norm* $|x|$ is the real number Max $\{|x_1|, \cdots, |x_i|, \cdots, |x_m|\}$, i.e., the greatest of the absolute values of its coordinates. Let k be a non-negative real number; the set $K = \{x \in R^m \mid |x| \leq k\}$ is a closed *cube* of R^m with *center* 0, *edge* $2k$.

s. A subset S of R^m is said to be *bounded* if it is contained in some closed cube K. A set which is *unbounded* is therefore a set which has points arbitrarily far from the origin.

EXAMPLE: The set J of integers (a subset of R) is unbounded.

t. A subset S of R^m is said to be *compact* if it is closed and bounded. It is easily proved that:

(7) *If $S_1, \cdots, S_j, \cdots, S_n$ are closed (resp. compact) subsets of $R^{m_1}, \cdots,$ $R^{m_j}, \cdots, R^{m_n}$, then $S_1 \times \cdots \times S_j \times \cdots \times S_n$ is a closed (resp. compact)* *subset of $R^{\sum\limits_{j=1}^{n} m_j}$.*

u. Finally, a subset S of R^m is said to be *connected* if it is *not* the union of two non-empty, disjoint subsets closed in S. In other words, a set S is connected if it cannot be partitioned into two non-empty subsets closed in S, i.e., loosely speaking, if it is of one piece (but perhaps with holes). One can prove that:

(8) *A subset of R is connected if and only if it is an interval.*

1.7. Continuous Functions

N.B.   *a.* In this section, S denotes a subset of R^m, T a subset of R^n, (x^q) a sequence of points of S, and (y^q) a sequence of points of T.

b. Let f be a function from S to T, and consider a point $x^0 \in S$. The function f is *continuous at the point* x^0 if:

$$\text{``} x^q \to x^0,\; y^0 = f(x^0),\; y^q = f(x^q) \text{''} \quad \text{implies} \quad \text{``} y^q \to y^0. \text{''}$$

In other words, f is continuous at x^0 if the image of *any* sequence tending to x^0 is a sequence tending to the image of x^0.

Example: Let f be the real-valued function of a real variable (i.e., a function from R to R) defined by $y = 1/x$ if $x \neq 0$, and $y = 0$ if $x = 0$. The function f is continuous at every point of R, with the exception of 0, as its graph readily suggests.

The function f is *continuous on S* if it is continuous at every point of S.

c. Let S_1, S_2, T be subsets of R^{m_1}, R^{m_2}, R^n respectively, f be a function from S_1 to S_2, and g be a function from S_2 to T. Define a function h from S_1 to T by $h(x) = g(f(x))$ for every x in S_1. It is immediate that:

(1) *If f is continuous at the point x of S_1, and if g is continuous at the point $f(x)$ of S_2, then h is continuous at x.*

d. For every $k = 1, \cdots, p$, let T_k be a subset of R^{n_k} and consider the product $T = \prod\limits_{k=1}^{p} T_k$. It is immediate that the projection on T_k (see 1.3.g) is continuous on T.

e. With the notations of the last paragraph, let f_k be a function from S to T_k and define a function f from S to T by $f(x) = (f_k(x))$ for every

x in S, where $(f_k(x))$ denotes the p-tuple $(f_1(x), \cdots, f_p(x))$. It is immediate that:

(2)   *If every f_k is continuous at the point x of S, then f is continuous at x.*

f. One can prove:

(3)   *A function from S to T is continuous on S if and only if the inverse image of every set closed in T is closed in S.*

g. In the important particular case where f is a *real-valued* function on S, i.e., where f is a function from S to R, one can prove:

(3′)   *A function from S to R is continuous on S if and only if the inverse image of every interval of R of the form* $]\leftarrow, y]$ *or* $[y, \rightarrow[$ *is closed in S.*

EXAMPLES: (1) Let R^+ be the set of positive reals, and consider the function f from $S = R \times R^+$ to R defined by $y = f(u, v) = u/v$. "The function f is continuous on S" is equivalent to "the inverse image of $]\leftarrow, y]$, i.e., the set $\{(u, v) \in S \mid u - yv \leqq 0\}$, is closed in S, and similarly for $[y, \rightarrow[$"; the second assertion is readily suggested by a drawing in R^2, and easily proved. (2) The example of 1.7.b does not satisfy the continuity criterion of (3′), as the graph shows.

h. One can prove:

(4)   *Let f be a function from S to T. If f is continuous on S, and if S is compact, then $f(S)$ is compact.*

i. Applying this result to the particular case where f is real-valued, one obtains immediately:

(4′)   (Weierstrass) *Let f be a function from S to R. If f is continuous on S, and if S is compact, non-empty, then $f(S)$ has a maximum and a minimum.*

"$f(S)$ has a maximum" also means (1.5.g) "there is an x^M in S such that for all $x \in S$ one has $f(x) \leqq f(x^M)$." Such an element is called a *maximizer* of f. The concept of a *minimizer* is similarly introduced. The maximum (resp. minimum) of the set $f(S)$ is also called the *maximum* (resp. *minimum*) *of the function f on S.*

EXAMPLE: Let f be the function defined in the example of 1.7.b, and I an interval to which the variable x is restricted. One sees on the graph of f how, when I is not bounded, or not closed, or owns 0 and a different point, f has no maximizer or no minimizer.

j. It is easy to prove (using (3)),

(5)   *Let f be a function from S to T. If f is continuous on S, and if S is connected, then $f(S)$ is connected.*

k. Applying this result to the particular case where f is real-valued, one obtains immediately (see (8) of 1.6.u):

(5′) (Bolzano) *Let f be a function from S to R. If f is continuous on S, and if S is connected, then f (S) is an interval.*

Thus, if x^1, x^2 are two points of S, and y is a real number such that $f(x^1) \leq y \leq f(x^2)$, then there is an $x \in S$ such that $f(x) = y$. In other words, f takes on all values between $f(x^1)$ and $f(x^2)$. This result is often applied to the case where S is an interval of R.

1.8. CONTINUOUS CORRESPONDENCES

a. Example (2) of 1.3.h has pointed out the interest of correspondences for economics; this section will study their continuity.

N.B.   *b. In this section, S denotes a subset of R^m, T a compact subset of R^n, (x^q) a sequence of points of S, (y^q) a sequence of points of T, and φ a correspondence from S to T.*

c. The concept of continuity for a correspondence will be introduced in three steps.

d. Let x^0 be a point of S; one defines firstly:

The correspondence φ is *upper semicontinuous at the point* x^0 if:

$$\text{``} x^q \to x^0,\ y^q \in \varphi(x^q),\ y^q \to y^0 \text{''} \quad \text{implies} \quad \text{``} y^0 \in \varphi(x^0). \text{''}$$

In other words, if x^q tends to x^0, and if y^q tends to y^0 while belonging for all q to the image-set of x^q, one requires that y^0 belong to the image-set of x^0. One could also say, if x^q tends to x^0, and if the distance from y^0 to the image-set of x^q tends to zero, one requires that y^0 belong to the image-set of x^0. This is a natural but rather weak continuity requirement, as the following example shows. Let S and T be two compact real intervals. The graph of φ (fig. 2.a) is the shaded region, heavy-lined boundary included; $\varphi(x^0)$ is the interval $[a^1, a^2]$. The correspondence φ is upper semicontinuous at x^0.

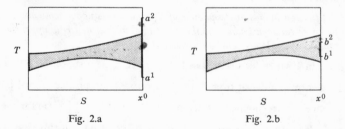

Fig. 2.a   Fig. 2.b

e. One defines secondly:

The correspondence φ is *lower semicontinuous at the point* x^0 if:

$$\text{``} x^q \to x^0,\ y^0 \in \varphi(x^0) \text{''} \quad \text{implies} \quad \text{``there is } (y^q) \text{ such that } y^q \in \varphi(x^q),\ y^q \to y^0. \text{''}$$

In other words, if x^q tends to x^0, and if y^0 belongs to the image-set of x^0, one requires that there be an infinite sequence (y^q) such that y^q tends to y^0 while belonging for all q to the image-set of x^q. One could also say, if x^q tends to x^0, and if y^0 belongs to the image-set of x^0, one requires that the distance from y^0 to the image-set of x^q tend to zero. Again, this is a natural but weak continuity requirement as the example of fig. 2.b shows. Here $\varphi(x^0)$ is the interval $[b^1, b^2]$. The correspondence φ is lower semicontinuous at x^0. Notice how the roles of "$y^0 \in \varphi(x^0)$" and "$y^q \in \varphi(x^q)$, $y^q \to y^0$" are permuted in the two preceding definitions.

f. Finally one defines:

The correspondence φ is *continuous at the point* x^0 if it is upper *and* lower semicontinuous at x^0.

φ then has all the desirable continuity properties at x^0.

g. When, for all $x \in S$, $\varphi(x)$ consists of a single element, the definition of lower semicontinuity at x^0 is obviously *equivalent* to the definition of continuity at x^0 for a function. One can prove that, in the same case, the definition of upper semicontinuity at x^0 is *equivalent* to the definition of continuity at x^0 for a function.

h. Semicontinuities and continuity *on S* are defined as semicontinuities and continuity at every point of S. It is clear that:

(1) *The correspondence φ is upper semicontinuous on S if and only if its graph is closed in $S \times T$.*

i. As in 1.7.c, let S_1, S_2, T be subsets of R^{m_1}, R^{m_2}, R^n respectively, f be a function from S_1 to S_2, and φ be a correspondence from S_2 to T. Define a correspondence ψ from S_1 to T by $\psi(x) = \varphi(f(x))$ for every x in S_1. It is immediate that:

(2) *If f is continuous at the point x of S_1, and if φ is upper semicontinuous (resp. lower semicontinuous) at the point $f(x)$ of S_2, then ψ is upper semicontinuous (resp. lower semicontinuous) at x.*

j. As in 1.7.d–e, for every $k = 1, \cdots, p$ let T_k be a subset of R^{n_k}, and φ_k be a correspondence from S to T_k. Consider the product $T = \prod_{k=1}^{p} T_k$, and define a correspondence φ from S to T by $\varphi(x) = \prod_{k=1}^{p} \varphi_k(x)$ for every x in S. If every T_k is compact, so is T by (7) of 1.6.t. In this case it is immediate that:

(3) *If every φ_k is upper semicontinuous (resp. lower semicontinuous) at the point x of S, then φ is upper semicontinuous (resp. lower semicontinuous) at x.*

k. According to example (2) of 1.3.h, the interest of these concepts for economics lies, in particular, in the interpretations of an element x of S as the environment of a certain agent, of T as the set of actions *a priori* available to him, and of $\varphi(x)$ (assumed here to be closed for every x in S) as the subset of T to which his choice is actually restricted by his environment x. Let f be a continuous *real-valued function on* $S \times T$, and interpret $f(x, y)$ as the gain for that agent when his environment is x and his action y. *Given x, one is interested in the elements of $\varphi(x)$ which maximize f* (now *a function of y alone*) on $\varphi(x)$; they *form a set $\mu(x)$.* What can be said about the continuity of the correspondence μ from S to T?

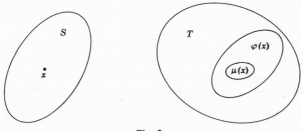

Fig. 3

One is also interested in $g(x)$, *the value of the maximum of f on $\varphi(x)$ for a given x.* What can be said about the continuity of the real-valued function g on S? An answer to these two questions is given by the following result (the proof of continuity of g should not be attempted).

(4)   *If f is continuous on $S \times T$, and if φ is continuous at $x \in S$, then μ is upper semicontinuous at x, and g is continuous at x.*

EXAMPLE: Let S and T be the real interval $[0, 1]$. Define φ by $\varphi(x) = [0, 1]$ for all $x \in S$, and f by $f(x, y) = xy$. For $x \neq 0$, $\mu(x)$ consists of the single element 1; for $x = 0$, $\mu(x) = [0, 1]$. For all x, $g(x) = x$. (It will be helpful to draw the graph of μ.)

l. Throughout this section, the assumption that T is compact has been made; it is essential in several respects. In applications, when the set T is not compact, one may still be able to replace T by some compact set without changing the problem, and thus to use the above results.

1.9. VECTORS IN R^m

a. Let $x = (x_i)$ and $y = (y_i)$ be two elements of R^m; one defines their *sum $x + y$* as $(x_i + y_i)$, i.e., the ith coordinate of $x + y$ is the sum of the ith coordinates of x and y. The element 0 has been defined (1.6.d) by the condition that all its coordinates are equal to 0. The *negative* of x is $-x = (-x_i)$. One writes $x - y$ for $x + (-y)$. If $x^1, \cdots, x^j, \cdots, x^n$ are n elements of R^m, their sum is denoted $\sum\limits_{j=1}^{n} x^j$.

b. Let $x = (x_i)$ be an element of R^m, and t a real number; one defines their *product* tx, or xt, as (tx_i). Geometrically, given two points x, y of R^m, one obtains $x + y$ by completing the parallelogram having $0x$, $0y$ for sides; one obtains $-x$ by taking the symmetric of x with respect to 0; one obtains tx by representing R on the straight line $0x$, choosing 0 to represent 0, x to represent 1; then $t \in R$ is represented by tx.

c. It is clear that the functions $(x, y) \to x + y$ from $R^m \times R^m$ to R^m, and $(t, x) \to tx$ from $R \times R^m$ to R^m are continuous.

d. The elements of R^m are also called *vectors*.

e. Given a vector a of R^m, the transformation of R^m into itself defined by $x \to x + a$ is called the *a-translation* in R^m.

f. Let X and Y be two subsets of R^m; one defines their *sum* $X + Y$ as the set of elements of R^m of the form $x + y$ where $x \in X$, $y \in Y$. In other words, one takes, in all possible ways, an element of X and an element of Y and adds them; the set of elements thus obtained is $X + Y$.

EXAMPLES: (1) Let $X = \{x \in R^2 \mid 0 \leq x_1 \leq 1, \ x_2 = 0\}$, and $Y = \{y \in R^2 \mid y_1 = 0, 0 \leq y_2 \leq 1\}$. Then $X + Y = \{z \in R^2 \mid 0 \leq z_i \leq 1, i = 1, 2\}$. (2) See also fig. 4 in R^2.

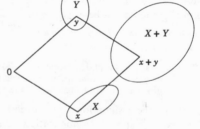

Fig. 4

One defines $-X$ as the set of elements of R^m of the form $-x$ where $x \in X$. One writes $X - Y$ for $X + (-Y)$. If $X_1, \cdots, X_j, \cdots, X_n$ are n subsets of R^m, their sum is denoted $\sum\limits_{j=1}^{n} X_j$. It is easy to prove :

(1) *If $X_1, \cdots, X_j, \cdots, X_n$ are n subsets of R^m, then $\sum\limits_{j} \overline{X}_j \subset \overline{\sum\limits_{j} X_j}$.*

That is, the sum of their adherences is contained in the adherence of their sum. One can also prove:

(2) *The sum of n compact subsets of R^m is compact.*

g. Let S be a subset of R^m, and for every $k = 1, \cdots, p$ let f_k be a function from S to R^n. Define a function f from S to R^n by $f(x) = \sum\limits_{k=1}^{p} f_k(x)$ for every x in S. It is immediate that:

(3) *If every f_k is continuous at the point x of S, then f is continuous at x.*

h. Similarly let S be a subset of R^m and for every $k = 1, \cdots, p$ let T_k be a subset of R^n, and φ_k be a correspondence from S to T_k. Consider the sum $T = \sum\limits_{k=1}^{p} T_k$, and define a correspondence φ from S to T by $\varphi(x) = \sum\limits_{k=1}^{p} \varphi_k(x)$ for every x in S. If every T_k is compact, so is T by (2). In this case one can prove (for lower semicontinuity the proof is immediate):

(4) *If every φ_k is upper semicontinuous (resp. lower semicontinuous) at the point x of S, then φ is upper semicontinuous (resp. lower semicontinuous) at x.*

i. Let x^1, x^2 be two points of R^m, t^1, t^2 two real numbers such that $t^1 + t^2 = 1$. The point $t^1 x^1 + t^2 x^2$ is called the *weighted average* of x^1 and x^2 with *weights* t^1 and t^2 (respectively).

j. Let x, y be two different points of R^m.

The *straight line* x, y is $\{z \in R^m \mid t \in R, z = (1 - t)x + ty\}$.

The *closed half-line* x, y (the *origin* x is written first) is $\{z \in R^m \mid t \in R, 0 \leq t, z = (1 - t)x + ty\}$.

The *open half-line* x, y is $\{z \in R^m \mid t \in R, 0 < t, z = (1 - t)x + ty\}$.

It may be more suggestive to rewrite the expression of z as $z = t(y - x) + x$, i.e., one multiplies the fixed vector $(y - x)$ by the variable number t; this gives the straight line (or the half-line) $0, (y - x)$; then one adds the fixed vector x (which amounts to a translation; see fig. 5 drawn for the case of the half-line).

k. Let x, y be two points of R^m (different or not). The *closed segment* x, y, denoted $[x, y]$, is $\{z \in R^m \mid t \in R, 0 \leq t \leq 1, z = (1 - t)x + ty\}$. (See fig. 5.) When $x = y$, the closed segment $[x, y]$ is said to be *degenerate*.

l. Given a subset C of R^m and a point x in C, C is said to be a *cone* with *vertex* x if it contains the closed half-line x, y whenever it owns the point y (different from x).

✓ *m.* Given n cones $C_1, \cdots, C_j, \cdots, C_n$ with vertex 0, they are said to be *positively semi-independent* if "$x_j \in C_j$ for every j, and $\sum_{j=1}^{n} x_j = 0$" implies "$x_j = 0$ for every j," i.e., if it is impossible to take a vector in each cone so that their sum is 0, unless they are all equal to 0. It is clear that two cones C_1, C_2 with vertex 0 are positively semi-independent if and only if $C_1 \cap (-C_2) = \{0\}$.

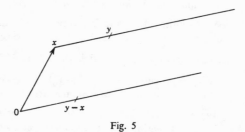

Fig. 5

n. Consider a subset S of R^m. To describe those of its points that are infinitely far from 0 one introduces the concept of its asymptotic cone, as follows. Let k be a non-negative real number, and denote by S^k the set $\{x \in S \,|\, |x| \geq k\}$ of vectors in S whose norm is greater than or equal to k. Let $\Gamma(S^k)$ be the least *closed* cone with vertex 0 containing S^k (i.e., the intersection of all the closed cones with vertex 0 containing S^k). The *asymptotic cone of S*, denoted $\mathbf{A}S$, is defined as the intersection of all the $\Gamma(S^k)$, i.e., $\mathbf{A}S = \bigcap_{k \geq 0} \Gamma(S^k)$; it is clearly a closed cone with vertex 0.

o. It is obvious that "$S_1 \subset S_2$" implies "$\mathbf{A}S_1 \subset \mathbf{A}S_2$." One can prove that:

(5)   *If S is a subset of R^m, and x is a vector in R^m, then* $\mathbf{A}(S + \{x\}) = \mathbf{A}S$.

In other words, a translation of S does not alter its asymptotic cone. It is then easy to prove that:

(6)   *If $T \neq \emptyset$ and S are two subsets of R^m, then* $\mathbf{A}S \subset \mathbf{A}(S + T)$.

One can also prove that:

(7)   *If, for every $j = 1, \cdots, n$, S_j is a subset of R^{m_j}, then* $\mathbf{A}(\prod_j S_j) \subset \prod_j \mathbf{A}S_j$.

p. It is now possible to give answers to the two important questions: When is the intersection of a collection of sets bounded? When is the sum of a finite number of closed sets closed? One can prove the intuitive result:

(8)   *Given a collection of subsets of R^m, if the intersection of their asymptotic cones is $\{0\}$, then their intersection is bounded.*

One can also prove:

(9)   *Given n closed subsets of R^m, if their asymptotic cones are positively semi-independent, then their sum is closed.*

This is a generalization of (2), since the asymptotic cone of a bounded set is $\{0\}$.

q. A subset of R^m is *convex* if it contains the closed segment $[x, y]$ whenever it contains the points x, y; in other words, if, whenever it contains the points x, y, it contains their weighted average with arbitrary positive weights. The set K in fig. 7.a, 7.b, or 7.c is convex. The graph of fig. 2.a or 2.b is not convex. The condition on a set that it be convex is crucial for economics.

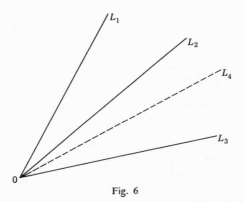

Fig. 6

r. A *convex polyhedral cone* is the sum of n closed half-lines.

Figure 6 pictures a convex polyhedral cone in R^3 which is the sum of four closed half-lines with origin 0. L_1 and L_3 are imagined to be in the plane of the page, L_2 in front of it, L_4 behind it.

s. It is easy to prove that:

(10)   *the intersection of a set of convex sets is convex,*

(11)   *the sum and the product of n convex sets are convex,*

(12)   *the adherence of a convex set is convex,*

and also, using (8) of 1.6.u, that:

(13)   *a convex set is connected.*

One can prove that:

(14)   *a closed, convex set owning* 0, *contains its asymptotic cone.*

t. Let S be a subset of R^m. Its *convex hull*, denoted $\overset{\cdot}{S}$, is defined as the intersection of all the convex sets containing S. According to (10), $\overset{\cdot}{S}$ is indeed convex and can therefore also be characterized as the smallest convex set containing S. One can prove that:

(15)   *Given n subsets of R^m, the convex hull of their sum is equal to the sum of their convex hulls.*

The *closed convex hull* of S is, by definition, the adherence $\overline{\overset{\cdot}{S}}$ of the convex hull of S. According to (3) of 1.6.j, $\overline{\overset{\cdot}{S}}$ is indeed closed; according to (12), it is indeed convex. It is easy to see that a closed convex set containing S necessarily contains $\overline{\overset{\cdot}{S}}$, which can therefore also be characterized as the smallest closed convex set containing S.

u. Let $x = (x_i)$ and $y = (y_i)$ be two elements of R^m; one defines their *inner product* $x \cdot y$ as the number $\sum_{i=1}^{m} x_i y_i$. It is clear that the function $(x, y) \rightarrow x \cdot y$ from $R^m \times R^m$ to R is continuous.

When $x \cdot y = 0$, one says that x and y are *orthogonal.* In the case of R^3, visualized as in 1.6.c, saying that two vectors x and y different from 0 are orthogonal is equivalent to saying that the half-lines 0, x and 0, y are perpendicular, provided that the units on the three axes have the same length.

v. Let p be an element of R^m different from 0, and c a real number; the set $H = \{z \in R^m \mid p \cdot z = c\}$ is a *hyperplane* with *normal p.* If z' is a point in H (one says also that *H goes through z'*), one has $p \cdot z' = c$ and the above expression may be rewritten $H = \{z \in R^m \mid p \cdot (z - z') = 0\}$. Thus the hyperplane H is the set of points z of R^m such that $z - z'$ is orthogonal to p; p and H are said to be *orthogonal.* If p and c are multiplied by the same real number different from 0, the hyperplane H is unchanged. An intersection of hyperplanes is called a *linear manifold.*

w. Given a hyperplane H with normal p, the point z of R^m is said to be *above H* if $p \cdot z > c$. The *closed half-space above H* is $\{z \in R^m \mid p \cdot z \geqq c\}$. One obtains similar definitions replacing *above*, $>$, $\geqq$ by *below*, $<$, $\leqq$. A closed half-space is easily seen to be closed and convex. So is a hyperplane, since it is the intersection of two closed half-spaces, and hence a linear manifold.

x. A hyperplane H is said to be *bounding* for a subset S of R^m if S is contained in one of the two closed half-spaces determined by H. In other words, H is bounding for S if S is entirely on one side of H with, possibly, points in it. One can prove the fundamental theorem:

(16) (Minkowski) *Let K be a convex subset of R^m and z a point of R^m. There is a hyperplane H through z and bounding for K if and only if z is not interior to K.*

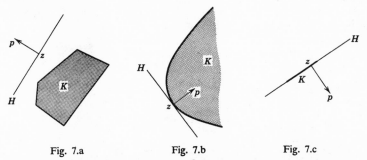

Fig. 7.a   Fig. 7.b   Fig. 7.c

The intuitive content of the result in R^2 is brought out by fig. 7.a, where z is exterior to K, by fig. 7.b, where z is in the boundary of K, and by fig. 7.c, where K (the heavy-lined segment) has no interior. It is easy to draw a non-convex set in R^2 for which some non-interior points are in no bounding hyperplane.

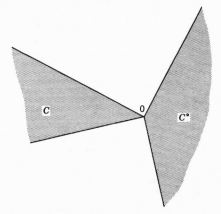

Fig. 8

y. Let C be a cone with vertex 0. Its *polar* is the set $C^\circ = \{x \in R^m \mid x \cdot y \leq 0 \text{ for every } y \in C\}$. It is easy to see that C° is a closed, convex cone with vertex 0.

Figure 8 provides an illustration in R^2.

z. According to the general convention of 1.4.j, an *ordering* is defined on R^m by $x \leqq y$ if $x_i \leqq y_i$ for every $i = 1, \cdots, m$. As remarked in 1.4.j, $x < y$ means "$x_i \leqq y_i$ for all i and $x_i < y_i$ for at least one i," and $x \ll y$ means "$x_i < y_i$ for all i." (Several authors have used the notation $\leqq$, $\leq$, $<$ respectively for $\leqq$, $<$, $\ll$.)

The *non-negative orthant* of R^m is the set $\Omega = \{x \in R^m \mid x \geqq 0\}$. The letter Ω has throughout this volume the meaning introduced here.

1.10. Fixed Points

a. Consider a set S and a function f from S to S, i.e., a transformation of S into itself. Great interest is attached to the existence of an element x' such that $x' = f(x')$, i.e., which coincides with its image, or which does not move in the transformation. Such an element is called a *fixed point* of the transformation f (see fig. 9.a).

b. One can prove the fundamental theorem:

(1) (Brouwer) *If S is a non-empty, compact, convex subset of R^m, and if f is a continuous function from S to S, then f has a fixed point.*

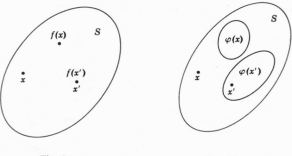

Fig. 9.a   Fig. 9.b

c. The generalization of this result to correspondences from a set to itself will play an essential role later on. Consider now a set S and a correspondence φ from S to S. A *fixed point* of the correspondence φ is an element x' such that $x' \in \varphi(x')$, i.e., which belongs to its image-set (see fig. 9.b).

d. One can prove:

(2) (Kakutani) *If S is a non-empty, compact, convex subset of R^m, and if φ is an upper semicontinuous correspondence from S to S such that for all $x \in S$ the set $\varphi(x)$ is convex (non-empty), then φ has a fixed point.*

NOTES

1. In a few cases the terminology and the notation adopted here are not the most common. Four of them call for comments.

The set $\{x\}$ and the element x are distinguished with care. Corresponding to these two different concepts, two different symbols, $\subset$ and ϵ, and two different locutions, "is contained in" and "belongs to," are used. Two different verbs are therefore used here to read $\supset$ and $\ni$: for the former "contains," and for the latter "*owns*," the natural counterpart of "belongs to."

A *correspondence* (N. Bourbaki's [1] term) has often been called a multi-valued function. Locutions such as these, where the object named by a noun and an adjective is not in the class of objects named by the noun alone, have been avoided here.

Preordering is N. Bourbaki's [1] term; *quasi-ordering* is G. Birkhoff's [1]. The most convenient way to denote a preordering is $\precsim$ (I. N. Herstein and J. Milnor's [1] notation), a juxtaposition of the two symbols $\prec$ for the derived asymmetric relation, and $\sim$ for the derived equivalence relation. Once the notation $\leqq$ has been adopted for the coordinate-wise ordering of R^m, the above principle leads to give to $x < y$ the meaning "$x \leqq y$ and $x \neq y$." The common usage of denoting this last relation by $x \leq y$ has therefore not been followed. As a consequence, $x \ll y$ is used, instead of $x < y$, to denote "$x_i < y_i$ for every i."

The somewhat awkward expression *positively semi-independent* has been created to describe the property of n cones introduced in 1.9.m.

2. The definition of R in 1.5.a–d raises the question: is there a set having all those properties? It is affirmatively answered by constructing the set J of non-negative and non-positive integers from the set N of positive integers, then the set Q of rationals from the set J of integers, and finally the set R of reals from the set Q of rationals (using either Cantor's or Dedekind's process). A set having all the properties of the text is easily seen to be unique (up to an isomorphism). Notice that, if the axiom $0 \neq 1$ is omitted, a one-element set satisfies the definition.

3. Most of the subjects treated in this chapter belong to the core of mathematics. For these no references are given. There are, however, three special topics for which a short bibliography may be necessary.

A study of the *continuity of correspondences* from a topological space to a topological space will be found in C. Berge [1], Chapter 6. The application of (4) of 1.8 made in G. Debreu [2] (with a different, and less satisfactory, terminology) may help to motivate the definitions and theorems of 1.8.

Results on *asymptotic cones* and references to the literature are given in W. Fenchel [1].

Theorem (2) of 1.10 on *fixed points of correspondences* is stated and proved in S. Kakutani [1]. It can be generalized in several directions; in particular the convexity assumptions on S and $\varphi(x)$ can be relaxed (see S. Eilenberg and D. Montgomery [1], E. Begle [1]).

CHAPTER 2

COMMODITIES AND PRICES

2.1. INTRODUCTION

The dual concepts of commodity and price are introduced in this chapter. The meanings of these terms, somewhat different from current usage, will be made precise in the next sections. Many examples will be given as illustrations.

It is possible to present in this introduction the essential features of the two concepts in a simplified and slightly imprecise manner. The economy is considered as of a given instant called the present instant. A commodity is characterized by its physical properties, the date at which it will be available, and the location at which it will be available. The price of a commodity is the amount which has to be paid *now* for the (future) availability of one unit of that commodity.

No theory of money is offered here, and it is assumed that the economy works without the help of a good serving as medium of exchange. Thus the role of prices is as follows. With each commodity is associated a real number, its price. When an economic agent commits himself to accept delivery of a certain quantity of a commodity, the product of that quantity and the price of the commodity is a real number written on the debit side of his account. This number will be called the amount paid by the agent. Similarly a commitment to make delivery results in a real number written on the credit side of his account, and called the amount paid to the agent. The balance of his account, i.e., the net value of all his commitments, guides his decisions in ways which will be specified in later chapters.

To link the preceding concept of price with the customary notion of an amount of money paid when and where the commodity is available, one must introduce the concept of price at a certain date, at a certain location. One obtains then, by comparing prices at the same location, at different

28

dates, interest, and discount rates; by comparing prices at the same date, at different locations, exchange rates.

In the next chapters the theory will be developed in terms of the two general, abstract concepts of commodity and price. To have concrete translations of its results one must use the present chapter, which provides a great variety of interpretations for the two concepts, as a key.

2.2. DATES AND LOCATIONS

i) elementary intervals   ii) elementary regions

The interval of time over which economic activity takes place is divided into a finite number of compact *elementary intervals* of equal length. These elementary intervals may be numbered in chronological order; the origin of the first one is called the present instant. Their common length, which may be a year, a minute, a week, ... is chosen small enough for all the instants of an elementary interval to be indistinguishable from the point of view of the analysis. An elementary interval will be called a *date*, and the expression "at date t" will therefore be equivalent to "at some instant of the tth elementary interval."

Similarly the region of space over which economic activity takes place is divided into a finite number of compact *elementary regions*. These elementary regions, which may be arbitrarily numbered, are chosen small enough for all the points of one of them to be indistinguishable from the point of view of the analysis. An elementary region will be called a *location*, and the expression "at location s" will therefore be equivalent to "at some point of the sth elementary region."

2.3. GOODS

The concept of a commodity can now be introduced by means of examples. The simplest is that of an economic *good* like wheat; it will be discussed in detail. There are indeed many kinds of wheat, and to have a well-defined good one must describe completely the wheat about which one is talking, and specify in particular its grade, e.g., No. 2 Red Winter Wheat. Furthermore wheat available now and wheat available in a week play entirely different economic roles for a flour mill which is to use them. Thus a good at a certain date and the same good at a later date are *different* economic objects, and the specification of the date at which it will be available is essential. Finally wheat available in Minneapolis and wheat available in Chicago play also entirely different economic roles for a flour mill which is to use them. Again, a good at a certain location and the same good at another location are *different* economic objects, and the specification of the location at which it will be available is essential. In the case now discussed a *commodity* is therefore defined by a specification of all its physical characteristics, of its availability date, and of its availability location. As soon as one of these three factors changes, a *different* commodity results.

The *quantity* of a certain kind of wheat is expressed by a number of bushels which can satisfactorily be assumed to be any (non-negative) real number. What is made available *to* an economic agent is called an *input* for him; what is made available *by* an economic agent is an *output* for him. For some agents inputs will be represented by non-negative numbers and outputs by non-positive numbers. For other agents the reverse convention will be made. A uniform convention might seem desirable, but a more flexible one will make interpretation easier. With one of the above conventions a quantity of wheat can be any real number.

Goods of the same type as wheat are cement, iron ore, crude rubber, wood pulp, cotton yarn, petroleum, water, gas, electricity (whose definition includes frequency and voltage, and whose quantity is expressed in kwhr), etc.

As the prototype of a second class of goods consider trucks. The complete description of this good includes model, mileage, . . . To define the corresponding commodity one must add its date and its location. A quantity of well-defined trucks is an integer; but it will be assumed instead that this quantity can be any real number. This assumption of perfect divisibility is imposed by the present stage of development of economics; it is quite acceptable for an economic agent producing or consuming a large number of trucks. Similar goods are machine tools, linotypes, cranes, Bessemer converters, houses, refrigerators, trees, sheep, shoes, turbines, etc.

Land requires special mention. Its condition is described by the nature of the soil and of the subsoil (the latter being of importance for construction work), the trees, growing crops and construction on it, etc. A quantity of land with specified condition, location, and date is expressed by a real number of acres.

Mineral deposits, oil fields, . . . are defined by a complete description of their content, their location, and, as always, their availability date. Their quantity is expressed by a real number of tons, barrels, . . .

2.4. SERVICES

The first example of an economic *service* will be human labor. Its description is that of the task performed; thus one has the labor of a coal miner, of a truck driver, of a member of some category of teachers, of engineers, of draftsmen, of executives, etc. (all including any further specification necessary for a complete description). When one adds date and location one has again a well-defined *commodity*. The *quantity* of a specified type of labor is expressed by the time worked (a real number).

Another type of service is illustrated by the use of a truck. It will be assumed that a truck (and similar economic objects) can be in only a finite number of distinguishable conditions. The life of a truck is described by a succession of time-intervals during each of which it stays in the same condition. The lengths of those intervals depend on the intensity of use. Thus the description of the service "use of a truck" is that of the truck (therefore of its condition during the time the service is rendered) and of the conditions under which it is used (mileage per day for example). One adds, as usual, date and location. The quantity of such a service is expressed by the time during which it is rendered.

A more complex type of service is illustrated by the use of a hotel room. The description of this service includes a listing of everything which will be performed for the occupant. It must, of course, be dated and located. Its quantity is an integral number of days; but it will again be assumed instead that this quantity can be any real number. Of the same type is, for example, the use of an apartment.

For other services, time is not the expression of the quantity. Such is a storage service which is described, for example, by the type of warehouse (refrigerated or not . . .), the dates from which to which it is rendered, and the location. Its quantity is expressed, for example, by a real number of cubic feet. One observes that in this case the temporal specification requires not one but several dates. Many other services, whose purpose is no longer to change the date of a commodity, require similarly more than one date to be temporally specified (at least when the elementary time-intervals are short enough), e.g., services of a repair shop, of a laundry, of a beauty parlor, attendance at a show, at a course, etc. In every one of these cases a unit is easily recognized; it is as always supposed to be perfectly divisible.

Finally, transportation services are described by the conditions under which they are rendered (rail, road, air, water, pipelines, power lines, etc., and any further specification necessary for a complete description), the locations they involve, and (since again they require a time longer than an elementary time-interval) the dates they involve. Their quantities are expressed for goods, for example, by the weight or the volume transported. For passengers the unit of the service is obvious. Temporal and spatial specifications of such services require several dates and several locations. Their quantities can, by assumption, be any real numbers.

2.5. COMMODITIES
i) commodity space

Summing up, a commodity is a good or a service completely specified physically, temporally, and spatially. It is assumed that there is only a finite number l of distinguishable commodities; these are indicated by an index h running from 1 to l. It is also assumed that the quantity of any one of them can be any real number. From now on the full generality of the concept of commodity, as illustrated by all the examples above, should always be kept in mind. By focusing attention on changes of dates one obtains, *as a particular case* of the general theory of commodities which will be developed below, a theory of saving, investment, capital, and interest. Similarly by focusing attention on changes of locations one obtains, *as another particular case* of the same general theory, a theory of location, transportation, international trade and exchange. The interpretation of the results in those terms will be left to the reader, since it offers no difficulty once the definition of a commodity has been grasped.

The space R^l will be called the *commodity space*. For any economic *agent* a complete plan of action (made now for the whole future), or more briefly an *action*, is a specification for each commodity of the quantity that he will make available or that will be made available to him, i.e., a complete listing of the quantities of his inputs and of his outputs. With one of the sign conventions of 2.3 an action is therefore represented by a point a of R^l.

2.6. PRICES

With each commodity, say the hth one, is associated a real number, its *price*, p_h. This price can be interpreted as the amount paid *now* by (resp. to) an agent for every unit of the hth commodity which will be made available to (resp. by) him.

The general term price covers a great variety of terms in current usage: prices proper, wages, salaries, rents, fares, fees, charges, royalties, . . .

Consider as an example the commodity No. 2 Red Winter Wheat available in Chicago a year from now. Its price is the amount which the buyer must pay *now* in order to have one bushel of that grade of wheat delivered to him at that location and at that date. Price as understood here is therefore very closely related to "price" as understood on a futures market. There a sale contract concerns a well-defined good to be delivered at a specified date, at a specified location. The "price" to be paid is also specified now (it is the "price" prevailing on the floor of the exchange), but it is understood that this "price" shall be paid *at the delivery date, at the delivery location*. This difference from the price concept which will be used here is inessential (see 2.7). A difference of another kind clearly exists. Organized futures markets concern only a small number of goods, locations, and dates (not too distant in the future), whereas it is implicitly assumed here that markets exist for *all* commodities.

The price p_h of a commodity may be positive (*scarce* commodity), null (*free* commodity), or negative (*noxious* commodity). In the last case an agent for whom that commodity is an output, i.e., who disposes of it, makes a payment to the agent for whom it is an input, i.e., receives from the latter a negative payment. The fact that the price of a commodity is positive, null, or negative is *not* an intrinsic property of that commodity; it depends on the technology, the tastes, the resources, . . . of the economy. For example, some industrial waste product may be a nuisance the disposal of which is costly; should an invention, i.e., a different technology, open uses for it, it might become a scarce commodity.

The *price system* is the *l*-tuple $p = (p_1, \cdots, p_h, \cdots, p_l)$; it can clearly be represented by a point of R^l. The *value* of an action a relative to the price system p is $\sum_{h=1}^{l} p_h a_h$, i.e., the inner product $p \cdot a$.

2.7. INTEREST, DISCOUNT, AND EXCHANGE

Imagine that a certain good circulates as money at location s, at date t, and let k be the index of the commodity thus defined. To obtain the price at s, at t of the hth commodity, $p_h^{s,t}$, i.e., the number of units of that money which must be paid at s, at t in order to have one unit of the hth commodity available, one would divide p_h by p_k. Doing this for all prices in p, one would obtain the price system at s, at t, $p^{s,t} = p(1/p_k)$. Instead of referring all prices to some money at s, at t, one might refer them, for example, to some good or service at s, at t. One is therefore led to the general concept of *price system at location s, at date t, $p^{s,t}$*, as derived from p by multiplication by a certain *positive* real number $\lambda^{s,t}$ (determined by the unit of value chosen at s, at t). In $p_h^{s,t}$ the location s and the date t correspond to payment, the location and date which are implicitly determined by h correspond to delivery; the first pair and the second are unrelated, in particular the payment date may be earlier than, simultaneous

33

with, or later than the delivery date. p now appears as the price system at an unspecified location, at an unspecified instant (of which it is often convenient to think as the present instant).

Let t^1, t^2 be two dates such that $t^1 < t^2$. The number $\alpha^s_{t^1,t^2}$ defined by $p^{s,t^2} = p^{s,t^1}\alpha^s_{t^1,t^2}$ is called the *accumulation factor at s from t^1 to t^2*. In this section p is always assumed to be different from 0; therefore $\alpha^s_{t^1,t^2}$ is a uniquely defined positive number. Its meaning is simple: by giving one unit of value at s, at t^1, one receives $\alpha^s_{t^1,t^2}$ units of value at s, at t^2. When, in particular, $t^1 = t$ and $t^2 = t + 1$, one defines the *interest rate at s from t to t + 1* by $i^s_{t,t+1} = \alpha^s_{t,t+1} - 1$. It is the difference between the value at s, at $t + 1$, one receives and the unit of value at s, at t, one gives. The interest rates usually quoted, e.g., .02 or 2%, are rates per annum; here all interest (and discount) rates are *rates per elementary time-interval*. From $\alpha^s_{t,t+1} = 1 + i^s_{t,t+1}$ one derives

$$\alpha^s_{t^1,t^2} = (1 + i^s_{t^1,t^1+1}) \cdots (1 + i^s_{t^2-1,t^2}),$$

a product of $t^2 - t^1$ terms. This prompts the definition of the *interest rate at s from t^1 to t^2*, $i^s_{t^1,t^2}$, as a certain average, by

$$\alpha^s_{t^1,t^2} = (1 + i^s_{t^1,t^2})^{t^2-t^1},$$

the positive root of $\alpha^s_{t^1,t^2}$ being taken.

Similarly the positive number $\beta^s_{t^2,t^1}$ defined by $p^{s,t^1} = p^{s,t^2}\beta^s_{t^2,t^1}$ is called the *discount factor at s from t^2 to t^1*. To receive one unit of value at s, at t^2, one gives $\beta^s_{t^2,t^1}$ units of value at s, at t^1. Clearly

$$\beta^s_{t^2,t^1} = \frac{1}{\alpha^s_{t^1,t^2}} = \frac{1}{(1 + i^s_{t^1,t^2})^{t^2-t^1}}.$$

One defines also the *discount rate at s from t^2 to t^1*, $d^s_{t^2,t^1}$, by

$$\beta^s_{t^2,t^1} = (1 - d^s_{t^2,t^1})^{t^2-t^1},$$

the positive root of $\beta^s_{t^2,t^1}$ being taken. For the hth commodity, $p^{s,t^1}_h = p^{s,t^2}_h\beta^s_{t^2,t^1}$ is called the price at s, at t^2 *discounted from t^2 to t^1*.

Let s^1, s^2 be two locations. The positive number ε^{s^2,s^1}_t defined by $p^{s^1,t} = p^{s^2,t}\varepsilon^{s^2,s^1}_t$ is called the *exchange rate at t, at s^1 on s^2*. One receives one unit of value at t, at s^2, by giving ε^{s^2,s^1}_t units of value at t, at s^1. For example, if the unit of value at New York (resp. London) is called dollar (resp. pound), the exchange rate at t at New York on London is the number of dollars at t (at New York) one pays for one pound at t (at London). One has

$$\varepsilon^{s^1,s^2}_t = \frac{1}{\varepsilon^{s^2,s^1}_t}.$$

In fact, the set of locations is partitioned into *nations*, and for all the locations s of a nation the price system at s, at a given date t, $p^{s,t}$, is the same (this statement is unrelated to the generally *false* statement that the same good or service available at t, at two different locations of a nation, has the same price). Then interest and discount rates, accumulation and discount factors are the same for all the locations of a nation, exchange rates are the same for all pairs of locations belonging respectively to a pair of nations; the nation only needs to be mentioned.

What has been said about the generality of the concept of commodity could be repeated now for the concept of price. It must always be remembered that when the price system p is known and the numbers $\lambda^{s,t}$ (p. 33) are given, all prices proper, wages, salaries, rents, fares, ... , all accumulation and discount factors, interest and discount rates, all exchange rates are determined at every date, at every location.

2.8. THEORY AND INTERPRETATIONS

To conclude this chapter it remains to sum up the formulation of all the above concepts in the language of the theory:

The number l of commodities is a given positive integer. An action a of an agent is a point of R^l, the commodity space. A price system p is a point of R^l. The value of an action a relative to a price system p is the inner product $p \cdot a$.

All that precedes this statement is irrelevant for the logical development of the theory. Its aim is to provide possible interpretations of the latter. Other interpretations will be presented in Chapter 7.

NOTES

1. The idea that a good or a service available at a certain date (and a certain location) is a different commodity from the same good or service available at a different date (or a different location) is old. The first general mathematical study of an economy whose activity extends over a finite number of elementary time-intervals under conditions of perfect foresight was that of E. Lindahl [1]. A similar treatment of time recurs in J. R. Hicks [1] (see also G. Tintner [1], [2]).

The use of negative prices originated in K. J. Arrow [1] and T. C. Koopmans [1].

2. The assumption of a finite number of dates has the great mathematical convenience of enabling one to stay within a finite-dimensional commodity space. There are, however, conceptual difficulties in postulating a predetermined instant beyond which all

economic activity either ceases or is outside the scope of the analysis. It is therefore worth noticing that many results of the following chapters can be extended to infinite-dimensional commodity spaces. In general, the *commodity space* would be assumed to be a vector space L over the reals and, instead of a price vector p, one would consider a linear form v on L defining for every action $a \in L$ its *value* $v(a)$. In this framework could also be studied cases where the date, the location, the quality of commodities are treated as continuous variables.

3. Two important and difficult questions are not answered by the approach taken here: the integration of money in the theory of value (on this point see D. Patinkin [1] and his references), and the inclusion of indivisible commodities.

CHAPTER 3

PRODUCERS

3.1. INTRODUCTION

An economy consists of a certain number of agents, the role of each of them being to choose a complete plan of action, i.e., to decide on the quantity of his input or of his output for each commodity. Thus an agent is characterized by the limitations on his choice, and by his choice criterion. This chapter studies a first class of agents, that of producers. The production plan of a producer is constrained to belong to a given set representing essentially his limited technological knowledge. In that set the production plan is chosen, for given prices, so as to maximize profit, the sum of all receipts minus the sum of all outlays. A natural program of work is thus suggested: to make precise from the viewpoint of the theory and from the viewpoint of interpretations the concepts of producer, of production plan, and of the set of possible production plans; to investigate the properties of such sets; then to introduce the profit maximization criterion; finally to study how the optimal production plans depend on prices.

3.2. PRODUCTIONS AND PRODUCTION SETS

In the study of production, when one abstracts from legal forms of organization (corporations, sole proprietorships, partnerships, . . .) and types of activity (Agriculture, Mining, Construction, Manufacturing, Transportation, Services, . . .) one obtains the concept of a *producer*, i.e., an economic agent whose role is to choose (and carry out) a production plan. It is assumed that there is a given positive integral number n of producers, and each one of them is indicated by an index $j = 1, \cdots, n$. *For a producer*, say the jth one, a production plan (made now for the whole future) is a specification of the quantities of all his inputs and all his

37

outputs; *outputs* are represented by *positive* numbers, *inputs* by *negative* numbers. With this convention a production plan, or more briefly a *production*, is represented by a point y_j of R^l, the commodity space. A given production y_j may be technically possible or technically impossible for the jth producer. The set Y_j of all the productions possible for the jth producer is called his *production set*. The point y_j is also called the *supply* of the jth producer.

The inputs of a production may include raw materials, semifinished products; land and equipment or their uses; labor of workers, foremen, executives, ... at various dates and locations. The outputs include, in general, more than one commodity, if only because the production involves several dates. The land, equipment, ..., which were inputs at one date may reappear as outputs at a later date, in a different condition. Generally, inputs and outputs together contain only a relatively small number of commodities, in other words most coordinates of y_j are null; this corresponds to the fact that Y_j is, in general, contained in a coordinate subspace of R^l with a relatively small number of dimensions. To the various types of activity correspond production sets with different characters.

A production y_j is classified as possible or impossible for the jth producer on the basis of his present knowledge about his present and future technology. The certainty assumption implies that he knows now what input-output combinations will be possible in the future (although he may not know now the details of the technical processes which will make them possible).

Given a production y_j for each producer, the sum $y = \sum_{j=1}^{n} y_j$ is called the *total production*, also the *total supply*. In forming this sum one cancels out all commodity transfers from producers to producers (each such transfer appears once as an output with positive sign and once as an input with negative sign); y describes therefore the *net* result of the activity of all producers together. That is to say, the positive coordinates of y represent outputs of producers not transferred to the production sector; the negative coordinates represent inputs of producers not transferred from the production sector. The set $Y = \sum_{j=1}^{n} Y_j$ (see 1.9.f) is called the *total production set*; thus $y_j \in Y_j$ for all $j = 1, \cdots, n$ is equivalent to $y \in Y$. The last set describes the production possibilities of the whole economy; it is, in general, no longer contained in a relatively small coordinate subspace of R^l.

Figure 1 illustrates the above concepts in the case where there are three commodities and two producers. The straight lines 0, 2 and 0, 3 are

imagined to be in the plane of the page, the straight line 0, 1 to be perpendicular to the plane of the page and pointing toward the reader. The
production set of the first (resp. second) producer is the closed half-line Y_1
(resp. Y_2) in the plane 1, 2 (resp. 2, 3). Then the total production set Y
is the shaded angle.

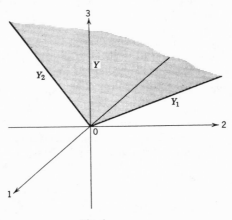

Fig. 1

In the language of the theory, this whole section is expressed as follows:

*The number n of producers is a given positive integer. Each producer is
indicated by an index $j = 1, \cdots, n$. The jth producer chooses a point, his
production or his supply y_j, in a given non-empty subset of R^l, his production
set Y_j. Given a production y_j for each producer, $y = \sum_{j=1}^{n} y_j$ is called the
total production or the total supply; the set $Y = \sum_{j=1}^{n} Y_j$ is called the total
production set.*

3.3. ASSUMPTIONS ON PRODUCTION SETS

All the assumptions on the sets Y_j which are used at one point or
another below, and others closely related, are discussed here. The order
in which they are listed corresponds approximately to decreasing plausibility.

(a) Y_j *is closed* (continuity),
i.e., let (y_j^q) be a sequence of productions; if all the y_j^q are possible for the
jth producer, and if $y_j^q \to y_j^0$, then y_j^0 is possible for the jth producer.

Narrowly related (see (1)) is the similar assumption for the total production set:

(a') *Y is closed.*

(b) $0 \in Y_j$ (possibility of inaction),
i.e., the *j*th producer has the possibility of doing nothing. The similar assumption for the total production set is:
(b') $0 \in Y$.

An economy where no production activity can take place is characterized by $Y = \{0\}$, i.e., the total production set consists of the single point 0.

(c) $Y \cap \Omega \subset \{0\}$ (impossibility of free production),
i.e., a possible total production whose inputs are all null has all its outputs null.

(d) $Y \cap (-Y) \subset \{0\}$ (irreversibility),
i.e., if the total production y, whose inputs and outputs are not all null, is possible, then the total production $-y$ is not possible. The productive process cannot be reversed since, in particular, production takes time and commodities are dated.

To prepare for the study of the next three assumptions, a few definitions are introduced here. Given a production y_j, to change the scale of operations is to multiply y_j by a non-negative number t. To increase (resp. decrease) the scale is to restrict further t to be larger than 1 (resp. smaller than 1).

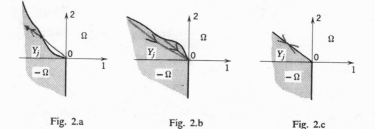

Fig. 2.a   Fig. 2.b   Fig. 2.c

Given Y_j, one says that:

non-decreasing returns to scale prevail if for any possible y_j one can arbitrarily increase the scale of operations,
non-increasing returns to scale prevail if for any possible y_j one can arbitrarily decrease the scale of operations,

40

constant returns to scale prevail if for any possible y_j one can arbitrarily change the scale of operations.

These three cases are illustrated respectively by figs. 2.a, 2.b, and 2.c.

(e) $(Y_j + Y_j) \subset Y_j$ (additivity),

i.e., if y_j^1 and y_j^2 are productions possible for the *j*th producer, so is $y_j^1 + y_j^2$. The sets Y_j in fig. 2.a and fig. 2.c have this property. In so far as Y_j represents technological knowledge, it is clear that two production plans separately possible are jointly possible. Alternatively the *j*th producer can be interpreted as an industry rather than as a firm; then the additivity assumption means that there is *free entry* for firms into that industry, i.e., no institutional or other barrier to entry. Under (e), if y_j is possible so is ky_j, where k is any positive *integer*. Therefore (e) implies a certain kind of non-decreasing returns to scale.

(f) Y_j *is convex* (convexity),

i.e., if y_j^1 and y_j^2 are productions possible for the *j*th producer, so is their weighted average, $ty_j^1 + (1 - t)y_j^2$, with arbitrary positive weights. Assumptions (f) and (b) together imply that, if y_j is possible, so is ty_j for every number t satisfying $0 \leq t \leq 1$; in other words, that non-increasing returns to scale prevail. The convexity assumption is crucial because of its role in all the existing proofs of several fundamental economic theorems. It is a limitation in that it rules out, when (b) holds, *increasing returns to scale* (i.e., non-decreasing returns to scale with the existence of a possible production for which the scale of operations cannot be arbitrarily decreased). But it still has a great generality since it is, in particular, weaker than the convex cone assumption which will be discussed in connection with (g).

Even if every Y_j is closed, Y is not necessarily closed. However,

(1) *If every Y_j is closed and convex, and if $Y \cap (-Y) = \{0\}$, then Y is closed.*

> *Proof:* According to (9) of 1.9.p it suffices to prove that the asymptotic cones $\mathbf{A} Y_j$ are positively semi-independent (1.9.m).
>
> It will first be shown that $\sum_j \mathbf{A} Y_j \subset Y$. Since $0 \in Y$, there is, for each j, a vector y_j^0 in Y_j such that $\sum_j y_j^0 = 0$. By (5) of 1.9.o and (14) of 1.9.s, one has $\mathbf{A} Y_j \subset Y_j - \{y_j^0\}$. The result follows by summation over j.
>
> It will now be proved that "$y_j \in \mathbf{A} Y_j$ for every j, and $\sum_j y_j = 0$" implies "$y_j = 0$ for every j." Consider one of them, $y_{j'}$. The vector

41

$\sum_{j \neq j'} y_j$ is in $\sum_j \mathbf{A} Y_j$, hence in Y; it is equal to $-y_{j'}$ which is similarly in $-Y$. If $y_{j'}$ were different from 0, a contradiction of $Y \cap (-Y) = \{0\}$ would result.

Closely related to (f) is the similar assumption for the total production set:

(f′)   *Y is convex.*

The latter is clearly weaker than the assumption "every Y_j is convex." Assumptions (f′) and (b′) together imply that non-increasing returns to scale prevail for the total production set.

(g) Y_j *is a cone with vertex* 0 (constant returns to scale),

i.e., if y_j is a production possible for the jth producer, so is $t y_j$, where t is any non-negative number. This assumption corresponds to the intuitive idea of an elementary production process for which the ratios of all outputs and all inputs to each other are fixed but the scale of operations can be arbitrarily varied.

Constant returns to scale (g) together with additivity (e) implies that Y_j is a *convex* cone with vertex 0. In the case of constant returns to scale, convexity is therefore easily justified. Note that, conversely, "convexity (f), additivity (e), and possibility of inaction (b)" implies "constant returns to scale (g)." Also, but this is of less interest, "convexity (f) and constant returns to scale (g)" implies "additivity (e)."

All the assumptions on Y_j listed so far ((a), (b), (e), (f), (g)), when made together, are equivalent to: Y_j is a closed, convex cone with vertex 0. Interesting particular cases are: Y_j consists of the single point 0; Y_j is a closed half-line with origin 0; Y_j is a convex polyhedral cone with vertex 0.

If every Y_j is a cone with vertex 0, so is Y.

(h) $Y \supset (-\Omega)$ (free disposal),

i.e., if a total production has all its outputs null, it is possible. In other words, it is possible for all producers together to dispose of all commodities. Closely related is the assumption:

(h′) $Y \supset (Y - \Omega)$,

i.e., if a total production is possible, so is one where no output is larger and no input smaller (in absolute value). Indeed it is easy to prove, for example, that "additivity (e) for Y and (h)" implies (h′); and, using (5) and (14) of 1.9, that

(2)   "*convexity* (f′) *for Y, continuity* (a′) *for Y and* (h)" *implies* (h′).

Finally, in a different connection, note that "free disposal (h) and irreversibility (d)" implies "impossibility of free production (c)."

3.4. PROFIT MAXIMIZATION

Given a price system p and a production y_j, the profit of the jth producer is $p \cdot y_j$. The total profit is $p \cdot y$.

Because of the sign conventions on the coordinates of y_j and p, the inner product $p \cdot y_j$ is indeed the sum of all receipts minus the sum of all outlays. Since commodities are dated, this concept of profit corresponds to the customary notion of the sum of all properly discounted anticipated future receipts minus the sum of all properly discounted anticipated future outlays. It is convenient to conceive of all producers as corporations, and to regard, for example, a sole proprietorship as a corporation with a single shareholder. One of the advantages of this viewpoint is that it makes clear that a sole proprietor usually plays two roles: that of a president of a corporation, in which capacity he receives an executive salary, and that of a shareholder, in which capacity he receives the profit.

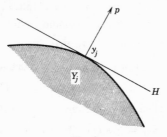

Fig. 3

It is assumed that each producer (a) considers prices as given (because, for example, his output or input of any commodity is relatively small and he thinks his action cannot influence prices) and (b) tries to maximize his profit. Choosing a production according to this principle amounts, for the producer, to distributing optimally over time and over space his inputs (investments for equipment, building, inventories, ..., labor, electricity, ...) and his outputs. In the language of the theory:

Given the price system p, the jth producer chooses his production in his production set Y_j so as to maximize his profit. The resulting action is called an equilibrium production of the jth producer relative to p.

When $p \neq 0$ one has the following geometric situation. If y_j is a maximizer, the set Y_j is contained in the closed half-space below the hyperplane H through y_j, with normal p (fig. 3). The set of maximizers is the intersection of Y_j and H.

Given an arbitrary p, there may be no maximum profit (for example, if non-decreasing returns to scale prevail, and if for some y_j in Y_j one has $p \cdot y_j > 0$, profit can be arbitrarily increased). Let therefore T_j' be the set of p in R^l for which the set of maximizers is not empty (T_j' is clearly a cone with vertex 0). Thus with each price system p in T_j' is associated the non-empty set $\eta_j(p)$ of possible productions maximizing profit for that p. The correspondence η_j from T_j' to Y_j is called the *supply correspondence of the jth producer*. The consideration of correspondences (instead of simpler functions) in the study of producers is inescapable for, in the important instance where Y_j is a closed convex cone with vertex 0, the set of maximizers consists of a single point only in trivial cases (see the end of this section). Let $\pi_j(p)$ be the maximum profit when the price system is p in T_j'. The function π_j from T_j' to R is called the *profit function of the jth producer*. If all the prices in p are multiplied by the same positive number t, clearly $\eta_j(tp) = \eta_j(p)$, i.e., the set of maximizers is unchanged, and $\pi_j(tp) = t\pi_j(p)$, i.e., the maximum is multiplied by t.

Given a price system p, there is a maximum profit for every $j = 1, \cdots, n$ if and only if p belongs to $\bigcap_{j=1}^{n} T_j'$. In that case one can define the non-empty set $\eta(p) = \sum_{j=1}^{n} \eta_j(p)$ of possible total productions compatible with profit maximization for that p by every producer. The correspondence η from $\bigcap_{j=1}^{n} T_j'$ to Y is called the *total supply correspondence*. One can also define the number $\pi(p) = \sum_{j=1}^{n} \pi_j(p)$. The function π from $\bigcap_{j=1}^{n} T_j'$ to R is called the *total profit function*. If t is a positive number,

$$\eta(tp) = \eta(p), \quad \text{and} \quad \pi(tp) = t\pi(p).$$

Summing up the above definitions for the sake of the theory (according to 1.3.c, $p \cdot Y_j$ denotes the image of the set Y_j by the function defined on R^l by $y_j \to p \cdot y_j$):

T_j' *is defined by* $T_j' = \{p \in R^l \mid p \cdot Y_j \text{ has a maximum}\}$. *The supply correspondence of the jth producer,* η_j, *from* T_j' *to* Y_j *is defined by* $\eta_j(p) = \{y_j \in Y_j \mid p \cdot y_j = Max\ p \cdot Y_j\}$. *The profit function of the jth producer,* π_j, *from* T_j' *to* R *is defined by* $\pi_j(p) = Max\ p \cdot Y_j$. *The total supply correspondence,* η, *from* $\bigcap_{j=1}^{n} T_j'$ *to* Y *is defined by* $\eta(p) = \sum_{j=1}^{n} \eta_j(p)$. *The total profit function,* π, *from* $\bigcap_{j=1}^{n} T_j'$ *to* R *is defined by* $\pi(p) = \sum_{j=1}^{n} \pi_j(p)$.

The following result is immediate:

(1) *Let $y_1, \cdots, y_j, \cdots, y_n$ be points of $Y_1, \cdots, Y_j, \cdots, Y_n$ respectively. Given p, $p \cdot y = Max\ p \cdot Y$ if and only if $p \cdot y_j = Max\ p \cdot Y_j$ for every j.*

In other words, y maximizes total profit on Y if and only if each y_j maximizes profit on Y_j. This is illustrated by fig. 4 and gives the simple characterization of $\eta(p)$ and $\pi(p)$:

(1') Given p in $\bigcap\limits_{j=1}^{n} T'_j$, $\eta(p) = \{y \in Y \mid p \cdot y = Max\ p \cdot Y\}$, and $\pi(p) = Max\ p \cdot Y$

In other words, $\eta(p)$ is the set of maximizers of total profit on Y; $\pi(p)$ is the maximum of total profit on Y.

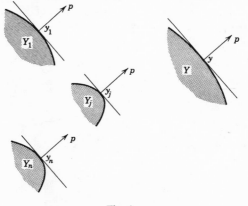

Fig. 4

In the rest of this section various assumptions on the production sets will be listed, and the implications of each one of them for profit maximization will be studied.

$0 \in Y_j$ (possibility of inaction). Given p in T'_j, 0 may be a maximizer (inaction may be optimal), it may even be the unique maximizer. In any case the maximum profit is clearly non-negative.

$(Y_j + Y_j) \subset Y_j$ (additivity). Given p in T'_j, the maximum profit is non-positive. (If a possible y_j gave a positive profit, $2y_j$ would also be possible and give a twice larger profit.) "Additivity and possibility of inaction" therefore implies that the maximum profit is null if it exists. This covers the case of a free entry industry.

45

Y_j *is convex* (convexity). Given p in T'_j, if $p = 0$, the set $\eta_j(p)$ of maximizers is Y_j itself; if $p \neq 0$, $\eta_j(p)$ is the intersection of Y_j and a hyperplane (see the discussion of fig. 3); in both cases $\eta_j(p)$ is convex. If every Y_j is convex, the set $\eta(p) = \sum\limits_{j=1}^{n} \eta_j(p)$ is convex for every p in $\bigcap\limits_{j=1}^{n} T'_j$, as a sum of convex sets.

Y_j *is a cone with vertex* 0 (constant returns to scale). Given p in T'_j, the maximum profit is null as in the case of "additivity and possibility of inaction." Therefore $T'_j = Y^\circ_j$, the polar of Y_j (1.9.y). The origin 0 is a maximizer; hence, if $p \neq 0$, the set $\eta_j(p)$ of maximizers is the intersection of Y_j and the hyperplane H through 0, orthogonal to p; if $p = 0$, the set $\eta_j(p)$ is Y_j itself. In both cases the set $\eta_j(p)$ is a cone with vertex 0. It is easy to prove that, when p belongs to the interior of Y°_j, the origin 0 is the unique maximizer (this is illustrated in R^2 by fig. 5.a). It is more

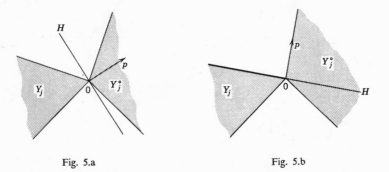

Fig. 5.a   Fig. 5.b

difficult to prove that, when p belongs to the boundary of Y°_j and Y_j is closed, the cone of maximizers is not reduced to the single point 0 (this is illustrated in R^2 by fig. 5.b; the cone of maximizers is the heavy closed half-line).

Every Y_j *is a cone with vertex* 0. Then so is Y. Given p, there is a maximum of $p \cdot y_j$ on Y_j for every j if and only if there is a maximum of $p \cdot y$ on Y (according to (1)). Therefore $\bigcap\limits_{j=1}^{n} Y^\circ_j = Y^\circ$, the polar of Y. Given p in Y°, the set $\eta(p)$ is, according to (1'), the set of maximizers of $p \cdot y$ on Y. What has just been said for $\eta_j(p)$ and Y_j can therefore be repeated for $\eta(p)$ and Y.

$Y \supset (-\Omega)$ (free disposal). Given p, there is a maximum of $p \cdot y_j$ on Y_j for every j only if there is a maximum of $p \cdot y$ on Y (according to (1)), hence only if $p \geqq 0$. Indeed, if $p_h < 0$, it would be possible to increase arbitrarily $p \cdot y$ by increasing (in absolute value) the total input of the hth commodity.

3.5. PRICE VARIATIONS

Let p be a first price system, and y_j a corresponding optimal production for the jth producer. If p' is a second price system, and y'_j a corresponding optimal production, then denote the price change $p' - p$ by Δp and the corresponding production change $y'_j - y_j$ by Δy_j. By definition $p \cdot y'_j \leqq p \cdot y_j$; hence

$$(1) \qquad\qquad p \cdot \Delta y_j \leqq 0.$$

Similarly $p' \cdot \Delta y_j \geqq 0$; therefore, by subtracting (1),

$$(2) \qquad\qquad \Delta p \cdot \Delta y_j \geqq 0.$$

If only one price varies, say p_h, (2) becomes

$$\Delta p_h \Delta y_{jh} \geqq 0,$$

where y_{jh} is the hth coordinate of y_j. Thus, if the price of a commodity increases, all other prices remaining constant, a producer increases or leaves unchanged his output of that commodity (decreases or leaves unchanged, in absolute value, his input of that commodity). By summation over j one obtains inequalities analogous to (1) and (2) for the total production:

$$(1') \qquad\qquad p \cdot \Delta y \leqq 0 \quad \text{and}$$

$$(2') \qquad\qquad \Delta p \cdot \Delta y \geqq 0.$$

It will be shown in 5.4, 5.7 how, under certain rather weak assumptions, the production set Y_j can be replaced by a certain non-empty *compact* subset of Y_j. The rest of this section will therefore study the case where Y_j is compact.

Given an arbitrary p, $p \cdot y_j$ defines a continuous function of y_j on Y_j, and (4') of 1.7.1 applies. Hence $p \cdot Y_j$ has a maximum. In other words, $T'_j = R^1$.

In fact, $p \cdot y_j$ defines a continuous function of (p, y_j) on $R^l \times Y_j$, and theorem (4) of 1.8.k applies (here the correspondence φ from R^l to Y_j

is defined by $\varphi(p) = Y_j$ for every $p \in R^l$; it is constant and thus trivially continuous). Hence η_j, the supply correspondence of the jth producer, *is upper semicontinuous on* R^l, and π_j, the profit function of the jth producer, *is continuous on* R^l.

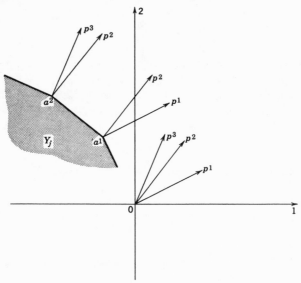

Fig. 6

Figure 6 makes intuitive the continuity properties of η_j and π_j. Consider a vector p rotating around 0 from p^1 to p^3. If p is interior to the angle $p^1 0 p^2$, then $\eta_j(p)$ consists of the single point a^1. If p is equal to p^2, then $\eta_j(p)$ consists of the closed segment $[a^1, a^2]$. If p is interior to the angle $p^2 0 p^3$, then $\eta_j(p)$ consists of the single point a^2.

When every Y_j is compact, according to (4) of 1.9.h, η, the total supply correspondence, *is upper semicontinuous on* R^l, and, according to (3) of 1.9.g, π, the total profit function, *is continuous on* R^l. Summing up:

(3) *If Y_j is compact, then* $T'_j = R^l$, η_j *is upper semicontinuous on* R^l, *and* π_j *is continuous on* R^l. *If every Y_j is compact, then η is upper semicontinuous on* R^l, *and* π *is continuous on* R^l.

When one of the upper semicontinuous supply correspondences η_j, η happens to be a function, it is *continuous* according to 1.8.g.

NOTES

1. K. Menger's [1] discussion of production functions (relating a single output to several inputs) contains definitions corresponding to non-decreasing, non-increasing, constant returns to scale, and additivity of 3.3. T. C. Koopmans' [1] basic study of convex polyhedral conic production sets introduces the impossibility of free production and irreversibility assumptions of 3.3.

Inequalities (1) and (2) of 3.5 are P. A. Samuelson's [1], Chapter 4.

2. Three phenomena that the present analysis does not cover must be emphasized: (1) *external economies and diseconomies*, i.e., the case where the production set of a producer depends on the productions of the other producers (and/or on the consumptions of consumers), (2) increasing returns to scale, (3) the behavior of producers who do not consider prices as given in choosing their productions.

CHAPTER 4

CONSUMERS

4.1. INTRODUCTION

This chapter studies a second class of agents, that of consumers. As in the case of a producer, the role of a consumer is to choose a complete consumption plan; he is characterized by the limitations on his choice, and by his choice criterion. Here the choice limitations are of two kinds: firstly, the consumption plan must satisfy certain *a priori* constraints (for example, of a physiological nature); secondly, given prices and the wealth of the consumer, the value of his consumption plan must not exceed his wealth. Under these limitations, a consumption plan to which none is preferred is chosen. The following natural program of work is thus suggested: to make precise from the viewpoint of the theory and from the viewpoint of interpretations the concepts of consumer, of consumption plan, of the set of *a priori* possible consumption plans; to investigate the properties of such sets; to make precise the concept of preferences among *a priori* possible consumption plans; to investigate the properties of preferences; next to introduce the wealth constraint; then to study the satisfaction of preferences under the two constraints (*a priori* possibility and wealth constraint); finally, to investigate the dependence of optimal consumption plans on prices and wealth.

4.2. CONSUMPTIONS AND CONSUMPTION SETS

A *consumer* is typically an individual, it may be a household, it might even be a larger group with a common purpose. His role is to choose (and carry out) a consumption plan made now for the whole future, i.e., a specification of the quantities of all his inputs and all his outputs. It is assumed that there is a given positive integral number m of consumers, and each one of them is indicated by an index $i = 1, \cdots, m$.

50

The *inputs* of the *i*th consumer are represented by *positive* numbers, his *outputs* by *negative* numbers. With this convention, his consumption plan, or more briefly his *consumption*, is represented by a point x_i of R^l, the commodity space. A given consumption x_i may be possible or impossible for the *i*th consumer; for example, the decision for an individual to have during the next year as sole input one pound of rice and as output one thousand hours of some type of labor could not be carried out. The set X_i of all the consumptions possible for the *i*th consumer is called his *consumption set*. The point x_i is also called the *demand* of the *i*th consumer.

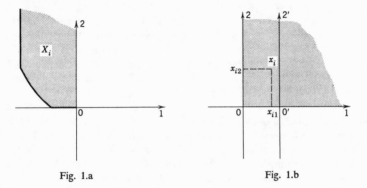

Fig. 1.a   Fig. 1.b

Many commodities do not, in general, enter into a consumption; this corresponds to the fact that X_i is generally contained in a coordinate subspace of R^l with a relatively small number of dimensions. Typically, the inputs of a consumption are various goods and services (related to food, clothing, housing, . . . , dated and located); its only outputs are the various kinds of labor performed (dated and located). The non-negativity of these inputs and the non-positivity of these outputs restrict further the set X_i. Finally, limitations of the rice-labor example type complete the determination of X_i. An individual who buys a house, a car, . . . for his own use and sells it back later plays two roles: that of a *producer* who buys and sells houses, cars, . . . in order to sell their services, and that of a *consumer* who buys the service, use of that house, of that car, . . .

Two examples will illustrate the above concepts for an individual consumer. First consider the case where there are one date and one location; a certain kind of labor defines the first commodity, a certain foodstuff (assumed to be freely disposable) defines the second commodity. X_i is represented by the shaded area in fig. 1.a.

51

Secondly, consider the case where there are one location and two dates; a certain foodstuff at the first date defines the first commodity, the same foodstuff at the second date defines the second commodity. Let the length of $[0, 0']$ (fig. 1.b) be the minimum quantity of the first commodity which that consumer must have available in order to survive until the end of the first elementary time-interval. If his input of the first commodity is less than or equal to this minimum, it might seem, on first thought, that his input of the second commodity must be zero. The set X_i would therefore consist of the closed segment $[0, 0']$ and a subset of the closed quadrant $1, 0', 2'$. Such a set has the disadvantage of not being convex in general. However, if both commodities are freely disposable, the set X_i is the closed quadrant $1, 0, 2$, which is convex: if the consumer chooses (perhaps because he is forced to) a consumption x_i in the closed strip $2, 0, 0', 2'$, it means that x_{i1} of the first commodity is *available to him* and he will actually consume at most that much of it, and that x_{i2} of the second commodity is *available to him* and he will actually consume none of it.

The two examples were restricted to the case of two commodities only to permit the use of diagrams. Their features are clearly general. The choice by the ith consumer of x_i in X_i determines implicitly his *life span*. Notice that the free disposal assumption which played an essential role in the second example, in restoring the convexity of X_i, is an assumption of free disposal for consumers' commodities only, and therefore much weaker than the total free disposal assumption (h) of 3.3.

This section can be summarized by:

The number m of consumers is a given positive integer. Each consumer is indicated by an index $i = 1, \cdots, m$. The ith consumer chooses a point, his consumption or his demand x_i, in a given non-empty subset of R^l, his consumption set X_i. Given a consumption x_i for each consumer, $x = \sum_{i=1}^{m} x_i$ is called the total consumption or the total demand: the set $X = \sum_{i=1}^{m} X_i$ is called the total consumption set.

4.3. ASSUMPTIONS ON CONSUMPTION SETS

All the assumptions on the sets X_i which are used at one point or another below are discussed here. The order in which they are listed corresponds approximately to decreasing plausibility.

(a) X_i *is closed* (continuity),
i.e., let (x_i^q) be an infinite sequence of consumptions; if all the x_i^q are

possible for the ith consumer, and if $x_i^q \rightarrow x_i^0$, then x_i^0 is possible for the ith consumer.

Narrowly related (see (1)) is the similar assumption for the total consumption set:

(a') *X is closed.*

(b) X_i *has a lower bound for* $\leq$ (lower boundedness),

i.e., there is a point χ_i in R^l such that $\chi_i \leq x_i$ for all x_i in X_i, or, in other words, such that $X_i \subset \{\chi_i\} + \Omega$. This assumption has an easy economic justification. If the hth commodity is an input, x_{ih} has a lower bound, zero. If the hth commodity is an output, i.e., a type of labor produced, there is clearly an upper bound (in absolute value) for the quantity of that labor which the consumer can produce during the corresponding elementary time-interval, whatever his other inputs and outputs may be.

The similar assumption for the total consumption set is:

(b') *X has a lower bound for* $\leq$.

If (b) holds for every X_i, then $\chi = \sum\limits_{i=1}^{m} \chi_i$ is a lower bound of X for $\leq$. Conversely, if X has a lower bound for $\leq$, then every X_i is easily seen to have a lower bound for $\leq$.

Even if every X_i is closed, X is not necessarily closed. However,

(1) *If every X_i is closed and has a lower bound for* $\leq$, *then X is closed.*

Proof: According to (9) of 1.9 it suffices to show that the asymptotic cones $\mathbf{A}X_i$ are positively semi-independent (1.9.m). Notice that $X_i \subset \{\chi_i\} + \Omega$ implies $\mathbf{A}X_i \subset \mathbf{A}(\{\chi_i\} + \Omega)$, and that, by (5) of 1.9.o, the last set is equal to $\mathbf{A}\Omega$, hence to Ω. Summing up, $\mathbf{A}X_i \subset \Omega$. Therefore it suffices to prove that "$x_i \in \Omega$ for every i, and $\sum\limits_{i=1}^{m} x_i = 0$" implies "$x_i = 0$ for every i," which is obvious.

(c) X_i *is connected* (connectedness).

This means, in an intuitive and imprecise language, that X_i is made of one piece (see the exact meaning in 1.6.u).

(d) X_i *is convex* (convexity),

i.e., if x_i^1 and x_i^2 are consumptions possible for the ith consumer, so is their weighted average, $tx_i^1 + (1 - t)x_i^2$, with arbitrary positive weights. As in the case of (f) of 3.3, this convexity assumption is crucial because of its role in all the existing proofs of several fundamental economic theorems. It can be intuitively justified by referring to the two examples discussed in connection with fig. 1.a and fig. 1.b.

According to (13) of 1.9 convexity (d) implies connectedness (c).

If every X_i is convex, then so is X.

4.4. PREFERENCES

Given two consumptions x_i^1, x_i^2 in X_i, one and only one of the following three alternatives is assumed to hold: for the ith consumer (a) x_i^1 is *preferred* to x_i^2, (b) x_i^1 is *indifferent* to x_i^2, (c) x_i^2 is *preferred* to x_i^1. It is most convenient to focus attention on the binary relation on X_i "is not preferred to," which may also be read "is at most as *desired* as." Clearly x_i is at most as desired as x_i for any x_i in X_i; moreover it is assumed that, for x_i^1, x_i^2, x_i^3 in X_i, "x_i^1 is at most as desired as x_i^2, and x_i^2 is at most as desired as x_i^3" implies "x_i^1 is at most as desired as x_i^3." The binary relation is thus reflexive and transitive; it is, according to the terminology of 1.4.b, a *preordering* which will be denoted $\underset{\sim}{\prec}_i$, and called the *preference preordering* of the ith consumer. It is, in fact, by the first assumption of this section, a *complete* preordering.

"$x_i^1 \underset{\sim}{\prec}_i x_i^2$ and $x_i^2 \underset{\sim}{\prec}_i x_i^1$" is denoted "$x_i^1 \underset{i}{\sim} x_i^2$" and read "$x_i^1$ is indifferent to x_i^2."

"$x_i^1 \underset{\sim}{\succ}_i x_i^2$ and not $x_i^2 \underset{\sim}{\succ}_i x_i^1$" is denoted "$x_i^1 \underset{i}{\succ} x_i^2$ and read "x_i^1 is preferred to x_i^2."

The binary relation $\underset{i}{\sim}$ on X_i is called the *indifference relation* of the ith consumer. It is obviously reflexive and transitive; it is also *symmetric*, i.e., "$x_i^1 \underset{i}{\sim} x_i^2$" implies "$x_i^2 \underset{i}{\sim} x_i^1$." Given a consumption x_i' in X_i, the set $\{x_i \in X_i \mid x_i \underset{i}{\sim} x_i'\}$, i.e., the set of consumptions in X_i which are indifferent to x_i', is called the *indifference class* of x_i'. It is easy to see that an arbitrary consumption in X_i belongs to one and only one indifference class. In other words, the set of indifference classes forms a partition of X_i.

A point x_i in X_i is called a *satiation* consumption if no possible consumption is preferred to it by the ith consumer.

The preference preordering of the ith consumer completely expresses his tastes with regard to food, clothing, housing, . . . , labor and also to consumption at some date or some location rather than at another. The preferences considered here take no account of the resale value of commodities; the ith consumer is interested in these only for the sake of the personal use he is going to make of them.

The above concepts will be illustrated by two examples. In the first one (fig. 2.a) there are one date, one location, two commodities; the set X_i is the closed quadrant 1, 0, 2. With each point of the closed half-line 0, 1 is associated its indifference class represented by a curve starting from that point. Four specimens have been drawn. The set of points preferred to a point x_i' of X_i is the set of points above the indifference curve of x_i'.

The second example is that which has been studied in connection with fig. 1.b (in 4.2). The indifference class of a point of $0, 0'$ is the closed vertical half-line from that point; three specimens of indifference curves of points of $0'$, 1 have been drawn.

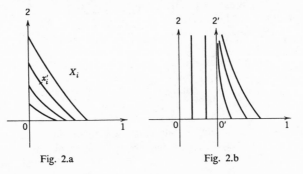

Fig. 2.a   Fig. 2.b

In the language of the theory, this section is expressed by:

The preference preordering of the ith consumer is a given complete preordering, $\underset{i}{\precsim}$, *on X_i. Given a consumption x_i' in X_i, the set $\{x_i \in X_i \mid x_i \underset{i}{\tilde{\succ}} x_i'\}$ is called the indifference class of x_i'. A greatest element of X_i for $\underset{i}{\precsim}$ is called a satiation consumption.*

All the assumptions on the preference preorderings $\underset{i}{\precsim}$ which are used at one point or another below are discussed in the next three sections: insatiability in 4.5, continuity in 4.6, convexity in 4.7.

4.5. INSATIABILITY ASSUMPTION ON PREFERENCES

(a) *No satiation consumption exists for the ith consumer,*
i.e., no matter what his consumption is (in X_i), there is another one (in X_i) which the ith consumer prefers.

4.6. CONTINUITY ASSUMPTION ON PREFERENCES

The consumption set X_i is partitioned into indifference classes. Is it possible to associate with each class a real number in such a way that, if a class is preferred to another, the number of the first is greater than the number of the second? In other words, given a set completely preordered by preferences, does there exist an increasing (1.4.k) real-valued function on that set? Such a function is called a *utility function*, and denoted u_i. The answer to the existence question is: not necessarily so (see an example in note 2). The main object of this section will therefore be to give an assumption on preferences (assumption (a)) from which the existence of a utility function can be proved (theorem (1)). In fact, this function would be of little interest if it were not continuous; the assumption on preferences should therefore enable one to prove that there is a *continuous* utility function on X_i.

The existence problem will be left aside for a moment, and the concept of a utility function will be discussed further. If u_i^1 is a utility function, and if f is an *increasing* function from R to R, the function u_i^2, defined on X_i by $u_i^2(x_i) = f(u_i^1(x_i))$ for all x_i, is clearly also a utility function. (If u_i^1 and f are continuous, u_i^2 is continuous by (1) of 1.7.) Given a preference preordering, a corresponding utility function is thus arbitrary to a large extent.

A utility function is a valuable tool in the proof of some results. It also gives a precise content to the intuitive notion of a numerical measure of how satisfied the ith consumer is with x_i.

Summing up for the sake of the theory:

A utility function u_i for the ith consumer is an increasing function from X_i preordered by $\underset{i}{\precsim}$ to R.

The existence problem will now be studied and, for this, the following continuity assumption on preferences is first introduced:

(a) *For every x_i' in X_i, the sets $\{x_i \in X_i \mid x_i \underset{i}{\precsim} x_i'\}$ and $\{x_i \in X_i \mid x_i \underset{i}{\succsim} x_i'\}$ are closed in X_i,*

i.e., let (x_i^q) be a sequence of consumptions possible for the ith consumer; if all the x_i^q are at most as desired as x_i', and if $x_i^q \to x_i^0$ (a consumption in X_i), then x_i^0 is at most as desired as x_i'. And similarly when "at most as desired as" is replaced by "at least as desired as." If there is a continuous utility function on X_i, preferences satisfy assumption (a) by (3') of 1.7.

The rest of this section is devoted to the proof of the converse theorem:

(1) *Let X_i be a connected subset of R^l, completely preordered by $\underset{i}{\precsim}$. Under assumption (a) there is on X_i a continuous utility function.*

    Proof (to lighten notation the subscript i will be omitted in this whole proof; thus X will stand for X_i, $\precsim$ for $\underset{i}{\precsim}, \cdots$): The trivial case where all the points of X are indifferent can be immediately disposed of. Any constant real-valued function on X is a continuous utility function. This case will be excluded until the end of this section.

The proof is based on the existence of a countable subset D of X which is dense in X (1.6.n). In part 2, a well-chosen increasing real-valued function is defined on D. In part 3, this function is extended from D to X. In part 4, the function so defined on X is shown to be continuous. Part 1 supplies a useful preliminary result.

1. *A preliminary result.*

(2) If x' and x'' in X satisfy $x' \prec x''$, there is an x in D such that $x' \prec x \prec x''$.

To prove this, consider the two sets $X_{x'} = \{x \in X \mid x \precsim x'\}$ and $X^{x''} = \{x \in X \mid x'' \precsim x\}$. They are disjoint, non-empty, and, by (a), closed in X. Since X is connected, their union cannot (1.6.u) be X, hence

$$X_{x'} \cup X^{x''} \neq X.$$

Assume now that there were no x in D with the desired property; this would mean that $D \subset X_{x'} \cup X^{x''}$. By (2) of 1.6.h, $\overline{D}$, the adherence in X of D, would be contained in the adherence in X of the right-hand set. The latter, however, is closed since it is the union of two closed sets. Hence one would have $\overline{D} \subset X_{x'} \cup X^{x''}$, or, since $\overline{D} = X$,

$$X = X_{x'} \cup X^{x''}.$$

A contradiction would thus result.

2. *A utility function on D.*

The utility function to be defined on D will be denoted u'. Select then two real numbers a, b such that $a < b$.

If D has a least element x^α, one takes $u'(x^\alpha) = a$.

If D has a greatest element x^β, one takes $u'(x^\beta) = b$.

Remove from D all the elements indifferent to x^α or to x^β, and call D' the remaining set. By (2),

(3) D' has no least and no greatest element.

An increasing function from D' onto the set Q' of rationals of the interval $]a, b[$ is defined as follows. Since D' is countable, its elements can be ranked $(x^1, x^2, \cdots, x^p, \cdots)$; this ranking is unrelated to the preordering $\precsim$. Similarly Q' is countable, and its elements can be ranked $(r^1, r^2, \cdots, r^q, \cdots)$; this ranking is unrelated to the ordering $\leq$. The elements of D' will be considered in succession; with x^p will be associated an element r^{q_p} of Q' in such a way that the preordering is preserved, and that every element of Q' is eventually taken.

Consider x^1; take $q_1 = 1$ and $u'(x^1) = r^{q_1}$.

Consider x^2; the set D' is partitioned into the following sets: the indifference class of x^1, the intervals $]\leftarrow, x^1[$ and $]x^1, \rightarrow[$. Two cases may therefore occur:

if $x^2 \sim x^1$, take $q_2 = q_1$ and $u'(x^2) = r^{q_2}$;

if x^2 is in one of the two intervals, say $]\leftarrow, x^1[$, consider the corresponding interval, $]a, r^1[$, of Q' and select in it the rational of *least rank*, r^{q_2}; take $u'(x^2) = r^{q_2}$.

In general, consider x^p; the set D' is partitioned into the following sets: the indifference classes of $x^1, x^2, \cdots, x^{p-1}$ (the number of different sets so obtained is at most $p - 1$), the intervals of the form $]\leftarrow, x^{p_1}[$, or $]x^{p_m}, x^{p_{m+1}}[$, or $]x^{p_{p-1}}, \rightarrow[$ where $m < n$ implies $x^{p_m} \precsim x^{p_n}$ (the number of non-empty intervals so obtained is at most p). Two cases may occur:

if $x^p \sim x^{p'}$ where $p' < p$, take $q_p = q_{p'}$ and $u'(x^p) = r^{q_p}$;

if x^p is in one of the intervals, say $]x^{p'}, x^{p''}[$, consider the corresponding interval, $]r^{q_{p'}}, r^{q_{p''}}[$, of Q' and select in it the rational of *least rank*, r^{q_p}; take $u'(x^p) = r^{q_p}$.

It is clear that the function u' is increasing. It is easy to check that (2) and (3) with the least rank rational selection imply that every element of Q' is eventually taken.

3. *Extension from D to X.*

The utility function to be defined on X will be denoted u. If x' is an element of X, one writes $D_{x'} = \{x \in D \mid x \precsim x'\}$ and $D^{x'} = \{x \in D \mid x' \precsim x\}$.

If x is a least element of X, take $u(x) = a$.

If x is a greatest element of X, take $u(x) = b$.

In the other cases, consider $\mathrm{Sup}\, u'(D_x)$ and $\mathrm{Inf}\, u'(D^x)$. These two numbers will be shown to be equal.

(1) If x' is any element of D_x, and x'' any element of D^x, one has $x' \precsim x''$. Thus, if r' is any element of $u'(D_x)$, and r'' any element of $u'(D^x)$, one has $r' \leq r''$. From this, one derives easily $\mathrm{Sup}\, u'(D_x) \leq \mathrm{Inf}\, u'(D^x)$.

(2) One cannot have $\mathrm{Sup}\, u'(D_x) < \mathrm{Inf}\, u'(D^x)$, for then any rational between them would not be taken on by u'.

Take for $u(x)$ the common value of the Sup and of the Inf.

It is clear that, if $x \in D$, one has $u(x) = u'(x)$, and u is indeed an extension of u' from D to X; in particular, $Q' \subset u(X) \subset [a, b]$. It is easy to check that u is increasing.

4. *Continuity of u.*

It will be proved that, if c is any real number, the inverse image of $[c, \rightarrow[$ by u is closed in X. A similar proof would apply to $]\leftarrow, c]$. According to (3') of 1.7, u will thus be proved to be continuous on X. If t is a real number, one writes $X_t = \{x \in X \mid u(x) \leq t\}$ and $X^t = \{x \in X \mid t \leq u(x)\}$.

It is clearly sufficient to consider the case where c is in $]a, b[$. Then the interval $[c, \rightarrow[$ is the intersection of the intervals $[r, \rightarrow[$ where $r \in Q'$ and $r \leq c$. By taking the inverse images by u, one obtains (see (1) of 1.3.d) $X^c = \bigcap_{\substack{r \in Q' \\ r \leq c}} X^r$. Let x be a point of X such that

$u(x) = r$; $X^r = \{x' \in X \mid x \precsim x'\}$, which is closed in X by (a). Therefore X^c is closed in X as an intersection of sets closed in X. This completes the proof.

According to (5') of 1.7, $u(X)$ is an interval with origin a, extremity b. The number a (resp. b) belongs to $u(X)$ if and only if X has a least (resp. greatest) element.

4.7. Convexity Assumptions on Preferences

N.B.   *In this section, X_i is always assumed to be convex.*

Three alternative convexity assumptions on preferences, (a), (b), (c), are of interest:

In (a), (b), (c), x_i^1 and x_i^2 are two different points of X_i, t is a real number in $]0, 1[$.

(a)   If $x_i^2 \succsim_i x_i^1$, then $tx_i^2 + (1 - t)x_i^1 \succsim_i x_i^1$ (weak-convexity),

i.e., if a possible consumption x_i^2 is at least as desired as another x_i^1, then their weighted average with arbitrary positive weights is at least as desired as x_i^1.

This assumption is easily seen to be equivalent to:

(a')   *For every x_i' in X_i, the set $\{x_i \in X_i \mid x_i \succsim_i x_i'\}$ is convex*, and to:

(a'')   *For every x_i' in X_i, the set $\{x_i \in X_i \mid x_i \succ_i x_i'\}$ is convex.*

An indifference class is said to be *thick* if its interior *in X_i* (see 1.6.o) is not empty. Assumption (a) allows thick indifference classes.

Figure 4.a shows a preference preordering of X_i, the non-negative quadrant, satisfying (a). The shaded region is a thick indifference class; two specimens of non-thick indifference classes have also been drawn.

(b)   If $x_i^2 \underset{i}{\succ} x_i^1$, then $tx_i^2 + (1 - t)x_i^1 \underset{i}{\succ} x_i^1$ (convexity),

i.e., if a possible consumption x_i^2 is preferred to another x_i^1, then their weighted average with arbitrary positive weights is preferred to x_i^1.

When preferences are continuous, assumption (b) implies assumption (a). In a formal statement:

(1)   *Under (a) of 4.6, (b) implies (a).*

> *Proof*: Let x_i^1, x_i^2 be two points of X_i such that $x_i^2 \underset{\tilde{i}}{\succ} x_i^1$. It must be shown that the set $\{x_i \in [x_i^1, x_i^2] \mid x_i \underset{i}{\prec} x_i^1\}$ is empty. This set cannot consist of a single point since its complement in $[x_i^1, x_i^2]$ is the set $\{x_i \in [x_i^1, x_i^2] \mid x_i \underset{i}{\succeq} x_i^1\}$ which is *closed* by (a) of 4.6. Therefore, if the former set were not empty, it would own two different points x_i' and x_i'' (see fig. 3.a). However, $x_i^1 \underset{i}{\succ} x_i''$ implies, by (b), $x_i' \underset{i}{\succ} x_i''$, and $x_i^2 \underset{i}{\succ} x_i'$ implies, by (b), $x_i'' \underset{i}{\succ} x_i'$. A contradiction would thus obtain.

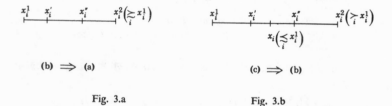

            (b) $\Rightarrow$ (a)   (c) $\Rightarrow$ (b)

            Fig. 3.a   Fig. 3.b

(b) is then actually stronger than (a), for it implies that a non-satiation indifference class is not thick. More precisely, as it is quite clear:

(2)   *Under (b), if x_i' in X_i is not a satiation point, x_i' is adherent to $\{x_i \in X_i \mid x_i \underset{i}{\succ} x_i'\}$.*

Assumption (b) allows indifference classes to contain non-degenerate closed segments.

Figure 4.b shows a preference preordering of X_i, the non-negative quadrant, satisfying (b). Five specimens of indifference classes have been drawn.

(c) *If* $x_i^2 \underset{i}{\sim} x_i^1$, *then* $tx_i^2 + (1 - t)x_i^1 \underset{i}{\succ} x_i^1$ (strong-convexity),

i.e., if the two possible consumptions x_i^1 and x_i^2 are indifferent, then their weighted average with arbitrary positive weights is preferred to them.

When preferences are continuous, assumption (c) implies assumption (b). In a formal statement:

(3) *Under (a) of 4.6, (c) implies (b).*

    Proof: Let x_i^1, x_i^2 be two points of X_i such that $x_i^2 \underset{i}{\succ} x_i^1$. Assume that there were x_i between x_i^1 and x_i^2 such that $x_i \underset{i}{\lesssim} x_i^1$ (see fig. 3.b). By (a) of 4.6 there is a continuous utility function u_i on X_i. There would therefore be a point x_i' between x_i^1 and x_i such that $u_i(x_i) < u_i(x_i') < u_i(x_i^2)$: if $x_i \prec x_i^1$, this is clear; if $x_i \underset{i}{\sim} x_i^1$, one applies (c). Because of the double inequality, there would be a point x_i'' between x_i and x_i^2 such that $u_i(x_i'') = u_i(x_i')$. From $x_i'' \underset{i}{\sim} x_i'$ and (c) would follow $x_i \underset{i}{\succ} x_i'$, a contradiction of $u_i(x_i) < u_i(x_i')$.

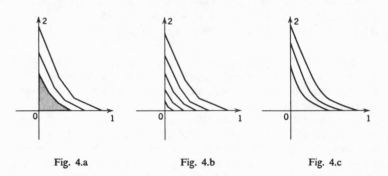

Fig. 4.a   Fig. 4.b   Fig. 4.c

(c) is then actually stronger than (b), for, as it is quite clear:

(4) *Under (c), an indifference class does not contain any non-degenerate closed segment.*

Figure 4.c shows a preference preordering of X_i, the non-negative quadrant, satisfying (c). Three specimens of indifference classes have been drawn.

Assumption (a) and even assumption (b) are intuitively justified; it is not so for assumption (c).

4.8. Wealth Constraint

Given a price system p and a consumption x_i, the *expenditure of the ith consumer* is $p \cdot x_i$. Because of the sign conventions on the coordinates of x_i and p, the inner product $p \cdot x_i$ is the sum of all outlays minus the sum of all receipts. Since commodities are dated, this concept of expenditure corresponds to the customary notion of the sum of all discounted future (proper) consumption outlays minus the sum of all discounted future labor receipts. The expenditure $p \cdot x_i$ must clearly be at most equal to the *wealth* of the ith consumer, a real number w_i. This concept of wealth corresponds to the customary notion of present value of everything (real estate, cars, furniture, . . . , stocks, bonds, . . .) the ith consumer owns, adding debts owed to him, subtracting debts he owes, . . . , each item being properly discounted. The m-tuple (w_i) is called the *wealth distribution*. It specifies the wealth of each consumer and can be represented by a point w of R^m. In the language of the theory:

Given the price system p and his wealth w_i, a real number, the ith consumer chooses his consumption x_i in his consumption set X_i so that his expenditure $p \cdot x_i$ satisfies the wealth constraint $p \cdot x_i \leqq w_i$. The point $w = (w_i)$ of R^m is called the wealth distribution. The point (p, w) of R^{l+m} is called the price-wealth pair.

When $p \neq 0$ one has the following geometric situation. The hyperplane $\{a \in R^l \mid p \cdot a = w_i\}$ is called the *wealth hyperplane*. The constraint $p \cdot x_i \leqq w_i$ expresses that x_i must be in the closed half-space below the wealth hyperplane (see for example fig. 7).

Given an arbitrary price-wealth pair (p, w), the set $\{x_i \in X_i \mid p \cdot x_i \leqq w_i\}$ in which the ith consumer must choose may be empty. Let therefore S_i be the set of (p, w) in R^{l+m} for which this is not so (S_i is clearly a cone with vertex 0). Thus with each price-wealth pair (p, w) in S_i is associated the non-empty set $\gamma_i(p, w) = \{x_i \in X_i \mid p \cdot x_i \leqq w_i\}$ of possible consumptions satisfying the wealth constraint for that pair (p, w). In this way a correspondence γ_i from S_i to X_i is defined. $\gamma_i(p, w)$ depends actually only on p and w_i; it has been presented in this form to prepare for the summation of individual demands which will be performed later. If t is a positive number, clearly $\gamma_i(tp, tw) = \gamma_i(p, w)$. Formal definitions are given for the sake of the theory:

S_i is defined by $S_i = \{(p, w) \in R^{l+m} \mid$ there is x_i in X_i such that $p \cdot x_i \leqq w_i\}$. The correspondence γ_i from S_i to X_i is defined by $\gamma_i(p, w) = \{x_i \in X_i \mid p \cdot x_i \leqq w_i\}$.

The rest of this section will study the continuity of γ_i. The definitions of 1.8.b–f apply only in the case where X_i is compact. It will be shown in 5.4, 5.7 how, under certain rather weak assumptions, the consumption set X_i can indeed be replaced by a certain non-empty *compact* subset of X_i. The following fundamental theorem will now be stated, discussed, and proved:

(1) *If X_i is compact, convex, and if (p^0, w^0) is a point of S_i such that $w_i^0 \neq Min\, p^0 \cdot X_i$, then γ_i is continuous at (p^0, w^0).*

In other words, given a compact, convex consumption set X_i and a price-wealth pair (p^0, w^0) in S_i, the correspondence γ_i is indeed continuous at the point (p^0, w^0) provided one rules out the exceptional case where $w_i^0 = Min\, p^0 \cdot X_i$, i.e., where the wealth w_i^0 is so small that for any smaller wealth there would be no possible consumption satisfying the wealth constraint.

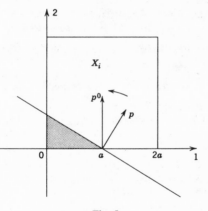

Fig. 5

Figure 5 shows how γ_i may not be continuous if $w_i^0 = Min\, p^0 \cdot X_i$. The set X_i is the closed square with edge 2. Consider $p^0 = (0, 1)$ and $w_i^0 = 0$; the corresponding wealth hyperplane is the straight line 0, 1. The exceptional case $w_i^0 = Min\, p^0 \cdot X_i$ occurs, i.e., there is no point of X_i below the wealth hyperplane. Let then a be the point $(1, 0)$, and let p, w_i tend to p^0, w_i^0 in such a way that the corresponding wealth hyperplane rotates around a as indicated in the figure. As long as $p \neq p^0$, the set $\gamma_i(p, w)$ is the shaded region whose limit is the closed segment $[0, a]$. However $\gamma_i(p^0, w^0)$ is the closed segment $[0, 2a]$.

The proof of existence of an equilibrium for a private ownership economy (5.7) will hinge upon the continuity of γ_i.

Proof of (1): The conditions of 1.8.b are clearly satisfied. It will therefore be proved that (1) γ_i is upper semicontinuous at (p^0, w^0), (2) γ_i is lower semicontinuous at (p^0, w^0).

(1)   The graph of γ_i is, by definition, $\{(p, w, x_i) \in S_i \times X_i \mid p \cdot x_i \leq w_i\}$. This set is clearly closed in $S_i \times X_i$. Hence, by (1) of 1.8.h, γ_i is upper semicontinuous *on* S_i.

(2)   Let (p^q, w^q) be a sequence of points of S_i tending to (p^0, w^0), and let x_i^0 be a point in $\gamma_i(p^0, w^0)$, i.e., $x_i^0 \in X_i$ and $p^0 \cdot x_i^0 \leq w_i^0$. One must prove that there is a sequence (x_i^q) of points of X_i such that $x_i^q \to x_i^0$ and, for all q, $x_i^q \in \gamma_i(p^q, w^q)$, i.e., $p^q \cdot x_i^q \leq w_i^q$. Two cases will be considered.

(2.1) $p^0 \cdot x_i^0 < w_i^0$. Hence, for all q larger than a certain integer q', $p^q \cdot x_i^0 < w_i^q$. The sequence (x_i^q) is defined as follows:

If $q \leq q'$, one takes for x_i^q an arbitrary point of $\gamma_i(p^q, w^q)$.
If $q > q'$, one takes $x_i^q = x_i^0$.

The sequence (x_i^q) clearly has all the desired properties.

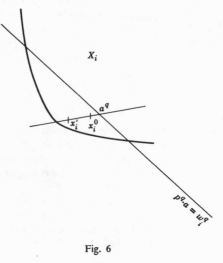

Fig. 6

(2.2) $p^0 \cdot x_i^0 = w_i^0$. By assumption, there is x_i' in X_i such that $p^0 \cdot x_i' < w_i^0$. Hence, for all q larger than a certain integer q',

$$p^q \cdot x_i' < w_i^q, \quad \text{and} \quad p^q \cdot x_i' < p^q \cdot x_i^0.$$

Consider the point a^q where the straight line x_i', x_i^0 intersects the wealth hyperplane determined by (p^q, w^q) (see fig. 6). For all q larger than q', a^q exists, is unique, tends to x_i^0, as it is easy to check. The sequence (x_i^q) is then defined as follows:

If $q \leq q'$, one takes for x_i^q an arbitrary point of $\gamma_i(p^q, w^q)$.
If $q > q'$ and $a^q \in [x_i', x_i^0]$, one takes $x_i^q = a^q$.
If $q > q'$ and $a^q \notin [x_i', x_i^0]$, one takes $x_i^q = x_i^0$ (because a^q might not be in X_i).

The sequence (x_i^q) clearly has all the desired properties.

4.9. PREFERENCE SATISFACTION

Given a price-wealth pair (p, w) in S_i, the ith consumer chooses, in the non-empty set $\gamma_i(p, w)$, a consumption x_i which is optimal according to his preferences, i.e., a greatest element for the preference preordering $\precsim_i$.

If there is a utility function u_i, one can also say that he chooses a maximizer of u_i on $\gamma_i(p, w)$ (in this case "preference satisfaction" is therefore synonymous with "utility maximization"). Doing this amounts to selecting the quantities of each good or service he will consume, and the quantities of each type of labor he will produce (at each date and location) which form a possible consumption plan optimal for his limited wealth. In the language of the theory:

Given the price-wealth pair (p, w) in S_i, the ith consumer chooses, in the set $\gamma_i(p, w)$, a greatest element for his preference preordering $\precsim_i$. The resulting action is called an equilibrium consumption of the ith consumer relative to (p, w).

When $p \neq 0$ one has the following geometric situation. If x_i' is a greatest element of $\gamma_i(p, w)$, the set $\{x_i \in X_i \mid x_i \underset{i}{\succ} x_i'\}$ has no point in common with the closed half-space below the wealth hyperplane H. Figure 7 illustrates the case where X_i is the non-negative quadrant. The indifference class of x_i' has been drawn as a broken line through x_i'. The set $\{x_i \in X_i \mid x_i \underset{i}{\succ} x_i'\}$ is the shaded region (indifference curve excluded).

If x_i' is an equilibrium consumption relative to (p, w), it is clearly a greatest element for $\underset{\sim}{\leq}$ of $\{x_i \in X_i \mid p \cdot x_i \leqq p \cdot x_i'\}$. It will be convenient to have the formal definition (which makes no reference to wealth):

The action x_i' is called an equilibrium consumption of the ith consumer relative to the price system p if it is a greatest element of $\{x_i \in X_i \mid p \cdot x_i \leqq p \cdot x_i'\}$ for $\underset{\sim}{\leq}$.

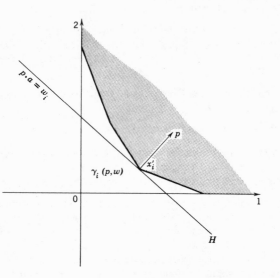

Fig. 7

Given an arbitrary pair (p, w) in S_i, $\gamma_i(p, w)$ may have no greatest element. Let therefore S_i' be the set of (p, w) in S_i for which the set of greatest elements of $\gamma_i(p, w)$ is not empty (S_i' is clearly a cone with vertex 0, the point 0 being excluded if and only if the ith consumer is insatiable). Thus with each price-wealth pair (p, w) in S_i' is associated the non-empty set $\xi_i(p, w)$ of possible consumptions optimal under the wealth constraint defined by (p, w). All the points of $\xi_i(p, w)$ are clearly indifferent. The correspondence ξ_i from S_i' to X_i is called the *demand correspondence of the ith consumer*. The use of correspondences in the study of consumers could be avoided only by making the strong-convexity assumption on preferences (c) of 4.7 for which there is little intuitive justification (see

66

section 4.7 and the last paragraph of the present section). Given two price-wealth pairs (p^1, w^1) and (p^2, w^2) in S'_i, (p^1, w^1) is said to be preferred (resp. indifferent) to (p^2, w^2) for the ith consumer if a point of $\xi_i(p^1, w^1)$ is preferred (resp. indifferent) to a point of $\xi_i(p^2, w^2)$. If there is a utility function u_i on X_i, the maximum utility, when the price-wealth pair is (p, w) in S'_i, is denoted by $v_i(p, w)$. The function v_i from S'_i to R is called the corresponding *indirect utility function of the ith consumer*. If t is a positive number, clearly

$$\xi_i(tp, tw) = \xi_i(p, w) \quad \text{and} \quad v_i(tp, tw) = v_i(p, w).$$

Given a price-wealth pair (p, w), there is a greatest element of $\gamma_i(p, w)$ for every $i = 1, \cdots, m$ if and only if (p, w) belongs to $\bigcap_{i=1}^{m} S'_i$. In that case one can define the non-empty set $\xi(p, w) = \sum_{i=1}^{m} \xi_i(p, w)$ of possible total consumptions compatible with the selection by every consumer of a consumption optimal for his wealth constraint. The correspondence ξ from $\bigcap_{i=1}^{m} S'_i$ to X is called the *total demand correspondence*. If t is a positive number, clearly $\xi(tp, tw) = \xi(p, w)$.

Summing up the above definitions for the sake of the theory:

S'_i *is defined by* $S'_i = \{(p, w) \in S_i \mid \gamma_i(p, w) \text{ has a greatest element for } \underset{\widetilde{i}}{\preceq}\}$.

The demand correspondence of the ith consumer, ξ_i, from S'_i to X_i is defined by $\xi_i(p, w) = \{x_i \in \gamma_i(p, w) \mid x_i \text{ is a greatest element of } \gamma_i(p, w) \text{ for } \underset{\widetilde{i}}{\preceq}\}$. *If there is a utility function u_i, the corresponding indirect utility function of the ith consumer, v_i, from S'_i to R is defined by* $v_i(p, w) = \text{Max } u_i(\gamma_i(p, w))$.

The total demand correspondence, ξ, from $\bigcap_{i=1}^{m} S'_i$ *to X is defined by* $\xi(p, w) = \sum_{i=1}^{m} \xi_i(p, w)$.

The analogy between fig. 7 and fig. 3 of 3.4 suggests that, given (p, w) in S'_i, x'_i is a greatest element of $\gamma_i(p, w)$ if and only if x'_i minimizes the expenditure $p \cdot x_i$ on the set $\{x_i \in X_i \mid x_i \underset{\widetilde{i}}{\succeq} x'_i\}$ of possible consumptions which are at least as desired as x'_i. The interest of such an equivalence would come in particular from the greater simplicity of the second operation and from its complete analogy with the maximization of the profit $p \cdot y_j$ on the set Y_j of possible productions; the theory of consumers and the theory of producers would thus be unified. The problem will now be formulated in a precise and slightly more general fashion.

In (a), (a'), (b), (b'), (p, w) denotes a given point of S_i, x_i' a given point of X_i, and x_i an arbitrary point of X_i.

Consider firstly the assumption:

(a) $p \cdot x_i \leqq w_i$ *implies* $x_i \underset{i}{\prec} x_i'$.

It is a generalization of the definition of x_i' as a greatest element of $\gamma_i(p, w)$ since the latter would require, in addition, that $p \cdot x_i' \leqq w_i$.

(a)   *is* (trivially) *equivalent to:*

(a') $x_i \underset{i}{\succ} x_i'$ *implies* $p \cdot x_i > w_i$.

Consider secondly the assumption:

(b') $x_i \underset{\widetilde{i}}{\succ} x_i'$ *implies* $p \cdot x_i \geqq w_i$.

It is a generalization of the definition of x_i' as a minimizer of expenditure on the set $\{x_i \in X_i \mid x_i \underset{\widetilde{i}}{\succ} x_i'\}$ since the latter would require, in addition, that $p \cdot x_i' = w_i$.

(b')   *is* (trivially) *equivalent to:*

(b) $p \cdot x_i < w_i$ *implies* $x_i \underset{i}{\prec} x_i'$.

Is then (a), (a') equivalent to (b), (b')? The answer is given by (1) and (2): (1) gives conditions under which (b) implies (a). And (2) gives conditions under which (a') implies (b').

In the remainder of this section various assumptions on the preference preorderings will be listed, and the implications of each one of them for preference satisfaction will be studied.

N.B.   *Until the end of this section, X_i is always assumed to be convex.*

The preference preordering $\underset{\widetilde{i}}{\prec}$ is continuous ((a) *of 4.6*).

Then expenditure minimization implies preference satisfaction provided the exceptional case $w_i = \text{Min } p \cdot X_i$, already met in 4.8, is excluded.

Figure 8 shows how the implication may not hold if $w_i = \text{Min } p \cdot X_i$. The set X_i is the closed quadrant 1, 0, 2. Three indifference lines have been drawn. Consider $p = (0, 1)$ and $w_i = 0$; the exceptional case occurs. The set $\gamma_i(p, w)$ is the closed half-line 0, 1, and the point $x_i' = (1, 0)$ is clearly not a greatest element of $\gamma_i(p, w)$ for $\underset{\widetilde{i}}{\prec}$. However, x_i' is a minimizer of expenditure on the set $\{x_i \in X_i \mid x_i \underset{\widetilde{i}}{\succ} x_i'\}$, represented by the shaded region.

The theorem can now be precisely stated and proved:

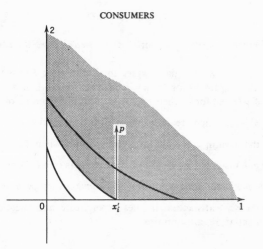

Fig. 8

(1) *If the continuity assumption (a) of 4.6 holds for $\underset{\sim}{\prec}$, and if $w_i = Min\ p \cdot X_i$ is excluded, then (b) implies (a).*

Proof: Since $w_i = Min\ p \cdot X_i$ is excluded, there is a point x_i^1 in X_i for which $p \cdot x_i^1 < w_i$. To prove the theorem it is sufficient to show that, if x_i^2 in X_i satisfies $p \cdot x_i^2 = w_i$, then $x_i^2 \underset{\sim}{\prec} x_i'$. For this, consider

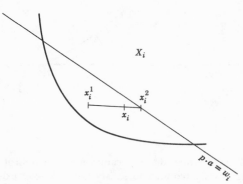

Fig. 9

any point x_i of the closed segment $[x_i^1, x_i^2]$, different from x_i^2. Clearly $p \cdot x_i < w_i$, hence, by (b), $x_i \underset{i}{\prec} x_i'$. Thus x_i^2 is adherent to the set $\{x_i \in X_i \mid x_i \underset{\sim}{\prec} x_i'\}$. As the latter is closed by (a) of 4.6, it owns x_i^2.

69

The preference preordering $\underset{\widetilde{i}}{\prec}$ satisfies the weak-convexity assumption (a) of 4.7.

Given a price-wealth pair (p, w) in S_i', the set $\xi_i(p, w)$ of possible consumptions optimal for (p, w) is convex. Indeed, if x_i' is a greatest element of $\gamma_i(p, w)$ for $\underset{\widetilde{i}}{\prec}$, then $\xi_i(p, w)$ is the intersection of $\gamma_i(p, w)$ and $\{x_i \in X_i \mid x_i \underset{\widetilde{i}}{\succ} x_i'\}$ which are both convex (for the second see (a') of 4.7).

When the assumption holds for every i, and when (p, w) is in $\bigcap_{i=1}^{m} S_i'$, the set $\xi(p, w)$ is convex as a sum of convex sets (see (11) of 1.9.s).

The preference preordering $\underset{\widetilde{i}}{\prec}$ satisfies the convexity assumption (b) of 4.7.

Then preference satisfaction implies expenditure minimization provided x_i' is not a satiation consumption.

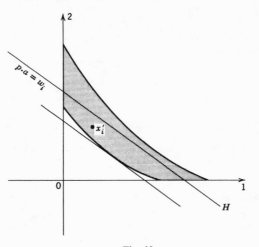

Fig. 10

Figure 10 shows how the implication may not hold if the preference preordering is only required to satisfy the weak-convexity assumption. The set X_i is the closed quadrant 1, 0, 2. A thick (see 4.7) indifference class has been represented by the shaded region. Let H be the wealth hyperplane. The point x_i' is a greatest element of $\gamma_i(p, w)$ for $\underset{\widetilde{i}}{\prec}$. It is clearly not a minimizer of expenditure on the set $\{x_i \in X_i \mid x_i \underset{\widetilde{i}}{\succ} x_i'\}$.

The theorem can now be precisely stated and proved:

(2) *If the convexity assumption* (b) *of 4.7 holds for* $\underset{\tilde{i}}{\prec}$ *and if* x_i' *is not a satiation consumption, then* (a') *implies* (b').

Proof: Since x_i' is not a satiation consumption, there is a point x_i^1 in X_i for which $x_i^1 \underset{i}{\succ} x_i'$. To prove the theorem it is sufficient to show that, if x_i^2 in X_i satisfies $x_i^2 \underset{\tilde{i}}{\succ} x_i'$, then $p \cdot x_i^2 \geqq w_i$. For this, consider

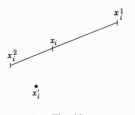

Fig. 11

any point x_i of the closed segment $[x_i^1, x_i^2]$, different from x_i^2. By (b) of 4.7, $x_i \underset{i}{\succ} x_i'$, hence, by (a'), $p \cdot x_i > w_i$. By continuity of $p \cdot x_i$ one obtains $p \cdot x_i^2 \geqq w_i$.

As a corollary:

(2') Given (p, w) in S_i', let x_i' be a greatest element of $\gamma_i(p, w)$ for $\underset{\tilde{i}}{\prec}$. If the convexity assumption (b) of 4.7 holds for $\underset{\tilde{i}}{\prec}$, and if x_i' is not a satiation consumption, then $p \cdot x_i' = w_i$.

Proof: By definition, one has $p \cdot x_i' \leqq w_i$. Since (b') holds by (2), and since, trivially, $x_i' \underset{\tilde{i}}{\succ} x_i'$, one has $p \cdot x_i' \geqq w_i$.

In other words, although the consumer is only constrained to satisfy the inequality $p \cdot x_i \leqq w_i$, the consumption x_i' he chooses satisfies the equality $p \cdot x_i' = w_i$. His expenditure equals his wealth. As a consequence, if (p, w') is in S_i', and if $w_i' > w_i$, the wealth w_i' is preferred to the wealth w_i.

The preference preordering $\underset{\tilde{i}}{\prec}$ *satisfies the strong-convexity assumption* (c) *of 4.7.*

Then, given (p, w) in S_i', there is clearly a *unique* greatest element of $\gamma_i(p, w)$ for $\underset{\tilde{i}}{\prec}$. In this case the demand correspondence ξ_i is a function. When the assumption holds for every i, so is ξ.

71

4.10. Price-Wealth Variations

N.B.   *In this section, it is always assumed that X_i is connected and that the preference preordering $\precsim_i$ is continuous ((a) of 4.6).* Hence there is on X_i a continuous utility function u_i ((1) of 4.6).

As remarked in 4.8, under certain weak assumptions, the consumption set X_i can be replaced by a certain non-empty *compact* subset of X_i. The case where X_i *is compact* will therefore be studied further.

Given a price-wealth pair (p, w) in S_i, the ith consumer maximizes the continuous function u_i on the set $\gamma_i(p, w)$ which is non-empty, compact. (4') of 1.7.i applies and the set of maximizers is not empty. In other words, $S'_i = S_i$.

In fact, u_i defines a continuous function u'_i on $S_i \times X_i$ by $(p, w, x_i) \rightarrow u_i(x_i)$, and theorem (4) of 1.8.k applies (here the correspondence φ from S_i to X_i is γ_i). Hence, if (p, w) is a point of S_i at which the correspondence γ_i is continuous, ξ_i, the demand correspondence of the ith consumer, *is upper semicontinuous at (p, w)*, and v_i, the indirect utility function of the ith consumer, *is continuous at (p, w)*.

When the above assumptions hold for every i, according to (4) of 1.9.h, ξ, the total demand correspondence, *is upper semicontinuous at (p, w)*. Summing up:

(1)   *If X_i is compact, then $S'_i = S_i$. If, in addition, γ_i is continuous at the point (p, w) of S_i, then ξ_i is upper semicontinuous at (p, w), and v_i is continuous at (p, w). If the above assumptions hold for every i, then ξ is upper semicontinuous at (p, w).*

When one of the upper semicontinuous demand correspondences ξ_i, ξ happens to be a function, it is *continuous* according to 1.8.g.

Notes

1.   The general concept of a consumption set and the lower boundedness assumption of 4.3 are borrowed from K. J. Arrow and G. Debreu [1]. I thank H. Lavaill and W. Vickrey for their remarks which helped me to formulate the determination of the life span in the second half of 4.2.

2.   About the history of utility theory, G. J. Stigler [1] may be consulted.

An example of a complete preordering which cannot be represented by a real-valued function is the *lexicographic* ordering of R^2. By definition, $(a, b) \prec (a', b')$ if (1) $a < a'$, or (2) $a = a'$ and $b < b'$. Assume that there is a real-valued representation f, and let

I_a denote the interval $[\text{Inf} f(a, R), \text{Sup} f(a, R)]$. Clearly that interval is non-degenerate, and $a \neq a'$ implies $I_a \cap I_{a'} = \emptyset$. Thus a one-to-one correspondence $a \leftrightarrow I_a$ is established between the set of real numbers (which is *uncountable*) and a set of pairwise disjoint, non-degenerate, real intervals (which is *countable*), a contradiction.

In the proof of (1) of 4.6, the assumption that X_i is a subset of R^l is used only to obtain a countable dense subset D of X_i. Therefore the following, more general, theorem has actually been proved. *Let X_i be a connected, separable topological space completely preordered by $\underset{\widetilde{i}}{\precsim}$. Under assumption* (a) *of 4.6 there is on X_i a continuous utility function.* In this form it is essentially a result of S. Eilenberg [1]. It may be worth noticing that the assumption of connectedness has been removed for spaces satisfying the second axiom of countability in G. Debreu [3] (and is thus superfluous in (1) of 6.2). The economic literature contains an earlier rigorous study of a particular case of the real representation of preferences, that of H. Wold [1].

Certain theorems whose statements list (a) of 4.6 among their hypotheses can, in fact, be proved by using weaker continuity assumptions on preferences inspired by I. N. Herstein and J. Milnor [1]. For example (denoting, for two points x_i' and x_i'' of X_i, the set $\{t \in R \,|\, tx_i'' + (1 - t)x_i' \in X_i\}$ by $T(x_i', x_i'')$), (1) of 4.9 uses only the assumption "for every x_i, x_i', x_i'' in X_i, the set $\{t \in T(x_i', x_i'') \,|\, tx_i'' + (1 - t)x_i' \underset{\widetilde{i}}{\precsim} x_i\}$ is closed in $T(x_i', x_i'')$"; (1) of 4.7 (and consequently (1) of 6.4) uses only the assumption "for every x_i, x_i', x_i'' in X_i, the set $\{t \in T(x_i', x_i'') \,|\, tx_i'' + (1 - t)x_i' \underset{\widetilde{i}}{\succsim} x_i\}$ is closed in $T(x_i', x_i'')$." These weaker assumptions are of special interest when the commodity space is infinite-dimensional, for they do not utilize the topology of X_i.

3. Earlier studies of the convexity assumptions on preferences (a), (b), (c) of 4.7 will be found in K. J. Arrow [1], G. Debreu [1], K. J. Arrow and G. Debreu [1]. If the continuity assumption (a) of 4.6 and the weak-convexity assumption (a) of 4.7 hold for preferences defined on a convex consumption set X_i, then these preferences can be represented by a continuous *quasi-concave* real function u_i ("quasi-concave" means that, for every real number a, the set $\{x_i \in X_i \,|\, u_i(x_i) \geqq a\}$ is convex). The problem of finding conditions under which a quasi-concave function can be transformed, by means of an increasing real function of a real variable, into a concave function has been investigated by B. de Finetti [1] and W. Fenchel [1].

4. Theorem (1) of 4.8 is essentially a result of K. J. Arrow and G. Debreu [1], theorem (1) of 4.9 a result of K. J. Arrow [1].

The concept of indirect utility function is due to H. Hotelling [1] and R. Roy [1], the term to H. S. Houthakker [1].

5. One would obtain inequalities similar to (1) and (2) of 3.5 by selecting for the ith consumer a consumption x_i' in his consumption set X_i, minimizing the expenditure $p \cdot x_i$ on the set $\{x_i \in X_i \,|\, x_i \underset{\widetilde{i}}{\succsim} x_i'\}$ for a given price system p, and then varying p.

6. It must be emphasized that the present analysis does not cover the case where the consumption set of a consumer and/or his preferences depend on the consumptions of the other consumers (and/or on the productions of producers).

CHAPTER 5

EQUILIBRIUM

5.1. INTRODUCTION

In order to obtain the central concept of an economy it remains only to introduce the total resources (the available quantities of the various commodities which are *a priori* given). To be precise, an economy is defined by *m* consumers (characterized by their consumption sets and their preferences), *n* producers (characterized by their production sets), and the total resources. A state of the economy is a specification of the action of each agent, and a state is said to be attainable if the action of each agent is possible for him and if their $(m + n)$ actions are compatible with the total resources. The set of attainable states plays an essential role; its properties are therefore studied. A special class of economies is then considered, namely, the private ownership economies where consumers own the resources and control the producers. Given a price system, each producer maximizes his profit, which is distributed to consumers-shareholders. The wealths of the latter are thus determined, and they satisfy their preferences under their wealth constraints. As a result of this process each agent chooses an action. These $(m + n)$ actions are not necessarily compatible with the total resources. Can one find a price system which makes them compatible? An answer is given in section 5.7 in the form of an existence theorem (for which the way is prepared by the result of section 5.6). This fundamental theorem of the theory of value explains the prices of all commodities and the actions of all agents in a private ownership economy.

5.2. RESOURCES

The *total resources* of an economy are the *a priori given* quantities of commodities that are made available to (or by) its agents. Quantities

74

made available to (resp. by) the agents of the economy are represented by positive (resp. negative) numbers. With this convention, the total resources are represented by a point ω of R^l, the commodity space. They include the capital of the economy at the present instant, i.e., all the land, buildings, mineral deposits, equipment, inventories of goods, ... now existing and available to the agents of the economy. All these are a legacy of the past; they are *a priori* given. The date of the commodities so defined is the first.

The total resources are a given point ω of R^l.

5.3. ECONOMIES ✓

A complete description of an *economy E* is now possible; it consists of:

For each consumer, his consumption set X_i and his preference preordering $\underset{\tilde{i}}{\precsim}$.

For each producer, his production set Y_j.

The total resources ω.

A *state* of the economy E is a specification of the action of each agent, i.e., for each consumer (resp. producer) a specification of his consumption x_i (resp. production y_j) in the commodity space. Thus a state of E is an $(m + n)$-tuple $((x_i), (y_j))$ of points of R^l. It can be represented by a point of $R^{l(m+n)}$. Formally:

An economy E is defined by: for each $i = 1, \cdots, m$ a non-empty subset X_i of R^l completely preordered by $\underset{\tilde{i}}{\precsim}$; for each $j = 1, \cdots, n$ a non-empty subset Y_j of R^l; a point ω of R^l.

A state of E is an $(m + n)$-tuple of points of R^l.

Given a state $((x_i), (y_j))$ of E, the point $x - y$ is called the *net demand*. In forming $x - y$ one cancels out all commodity transfers between agents of the economy (each such transfer appears once as an input with positive sign and once as an output with negative sign); $x - y$ describes therefore the *net* result of the activity of all agents together. That is to say, the positive (resp. negative) coordinates of $x - y$ represent inputs not transferred from (resp. outputs not transferred to) the agents of the economy. If $x_i \in X_i$ for every i, and $y_j \in Y_j$ for every j, the net demand $x - y$ belongs to the set $X - Y$.

Given a state $((x_i), (y_j))$ of E, the point $x - y - \omega$ is denoted z, and called the *excess demand*. It describes the excess of the net demand of all agents over the total resources. If $x_i \in X_i$ for every i, and $y_j \in Y_j$ for every j, the excess demand $x - y - \omega$ belongs to the set $X - Y - \{\omega\}$, which is denoted Z.

A state $((x_i), (y_j))$ of E is called a *market equilibrium* if its excess demand is 0. This can also be expressed by $x - y = \omega$, i.e., the net demand of all agents equals the total resources. The set of market equilibriums of E is a linear manifold in $R^{l(m+n)}$ denoted M.

A state $((x_i), (y_j))$ of E is said to be *attainable* if it satisfies the constraints:

(α) $x_i \in X_i$ for every i, $y_j \in Y_j$ for every j, $x - y = \omega$.

That is, the consumption of each consumer must be possible for him, the production of each producer must be possible for him, and the state must be a market equilibrium, i.e., the net demand must equal the total resources. The set of attainable states of E is a subset of $R^{l(m+n)}$ denoted A. According to (α):

(α') A is the intersection of $(\prod_i X_i) \times (\prod_j Y_j)$ and M.

Summing up:

Given a state $((x_i), (y_j))$ of E, the point $x - y$ is the net demand, the point $z = x - y - \omega$ is the excess demand. Z denotes the set $X - Y - \{\omega\}$.

A state $((x_i), (y_j))$ of E is a market equilibrium if $x - y = \omega$. The set of market equilibriums of E is denoted by M.

A state $((x_i), (y_j))$ of E is attainable if $x_i \in X_i$ for every i, $y_j \in Y_j$ for every j, $x - y = \omega$. The set of attainable states of E is denoted by A.

Given an economy E, a *consumption x_i for the ith consumer* is said to be *attainable* if there is an attainable state whose component corresponding to that consumer is x_i. The set of his attainable consumptions is called his *attainable consumption set*, and denoted $\hat{X}_i$. An *attainable production* for the jth producer and his *attainable production set* $\hat{Y}_j$ are similarly defined. According to the definition, $\hat{X}_i$ (resp. $\hat{Y}_j$) is the projection of A on the space R^l containing X_i (resp. Y_j). Formally:

Given an economy E, a consumption for the ith consumer (resp. a production for the jth producer) is attainable if it is the component corresponding to him of some attainable state. The set of his attainable consumptions (resp. productions) is his attainable consumption (resp. production) set, denoted by $\hat{X}_i$ (resp. $\hat{Y}_j$).

5.4. ATTAINABLE STATES

Various properties of the set A of attainable states of an economy E will now be studied.

It is clear that A is not empty if and only if $\omega \in X - Y$; this can also be written $0 \in Z$.

(1) *Given an economy E, if every X_i and every Y_j is closed, then A is closed.*

Proof: The product $(\prod_i X_i) \times (\prod_j Y_j)$ is closed. By (α') of 5.3, A is the intersection of two closed sets and is therefore closed.

If every set X_i and every set Y_j of an economy E is convex, so is A, for it is then, by (α') of 5.3, the intersection of two convex sets. Under the same assumptions, the sets $X - Y$ and Z are convex as sums of convex sets.

The sets X_i, Y_j of an economy E may be unbounded; but one expects, on account of the fixed resources ω, that the attainable consumption set of every consumer and the attainable production set of every producer be bounded, i.e., that A be bounded. This property of A will indeed play an essential role later on. Theorem (2) will therefore give conditions on the sets X, Y which insure that A is bounded. As an incidental result, conditions under which the set $X - Y$ (hence also the set Z) is closed will be obtained.

(2) *Let E be an economy such that X has a lower bound for $\leqq$, Y is closed, convex and $Y \cap \Omega = \{0\}$.*

If $n = 1$ and/or $Y \cap (-Y) \subset \{0\}$, then A is bounded.

If X is closed, then $X - Y$ is closed.

Proof: (1) To show that A is bounded, it suffices, according to (α') of 5.3 and (8) of 1.9, to prove that the intersection of the asymptotic cones $\mathbf{A}\left(\left(\prod_{i=1}^{m} X_i\right) \times \left(\prod_{j=1}^{n} Y_j\right)\right)$ and $\mathbf{A}M$ is $\{0\}$.

By (7) of 1.9, the first cone is contained in $(\prod_i \mathbf{A}X_i) \times (\prod_j \mathbf{A}Y_j)$; it is therefore sufficient to show that

(3) $\quad ((\prod_i \mathbf{A}X_i) \times (\prod_j \mathbf{A}Y_j)) \cap \mathbf{A}M = \{0\}.$

The cone $\mathbf{A}M$ is the linear manifold of states $((x_i), (y_j))$ satisfying the equality $x - y = 0$ since the latter set (1) is derived from M by a translation and hence has the same asymptotic cone as M, (2) is a closed cone with vertex 0 and hence coincides with its own asymptotic cone. Thus (3) is equivalent to:

(3') "$x_i \in \mathbf{A}X_i$ for every i, $y_j \in \mathbf{A}Y_j$ for every j, and $\sum_i x_i - \sum_j y_j = 0$" implies "$x_i = 0$ for every i, $y_j = 0$ for every j."

According to (6) of 1.9, one has $\mathbf{A}X_i \subset \mathbf{A}X$. Since X has a lower bound for $\leqq$, one has also, as seen in the proof of (1) of 4.3,

(4) $\qquad\qquad \mathbf{A}X \subset \Omega.$

Hence $\qquad\qquad \mathbf{A}X_i \subset \Omega$ and, consequently,

(5) $\qquad\qquad \sum_i \mathbf{A}X_i \subset \Omega.$

Similarly, one has $\mathbf{A} Y_j \subset \mathbf{A} Y$. Since Y is closed, convex, and owns 0, one has also, by (14) of 1.9,

(6) $\mathbf{A} Y \subset Y.$

Hence $\mathbf{A} Y_j \subset Y$ and, consequently,

(7) $\sum_j \mathbf{A} Y_j \subset Y.$

(3') can now be proved. According to (5), $\sum_i x_i \in \Omega$. According to (7), $\sum_j y_j \in Y$. Because of $Y \cap \Omega = \{0\}$, the relation $\sum_i x_i = \sum y_j$ thus implies $\sum_{i=1}^{m} x_i = 0 = \sum_{j=1}^{n} y_j$.

As "$\sum_{i=1}^{m} x_i = 0$ and $x_i \in \Omega$ for every i" implies "$x_i = 0$ for every i," the proof is completed in the case $n = 1$.

If $Y \cap (-Y) \subset \{0\}$, one shows, exactly as for (1) of 3.3, that $\sum_{j=1}^{n} y_j = 0$ implies "$y_j = 0$ for every j." And the proof is also completed in this case.

(2) To show that $X - Y$ is closed, it suffices, according to (9) of 1.9, to prove that the asymptotic cones $\mathbf{A} X$ and $\mathbf{A}(-Y)$ are positively semi-independent. But this is equivalent to $\mathbf{A} X \cap \mathbf{A} Y = \{0\}$, which follows directly from (4), (6), and $Y \cap \Omega = \{0\}$.

Since the ith attainable consumption set $\hat{X}_i$ (resp. the jth attainable production set $\hat{Y}_j$) of an economy E is the projection of A on the space R^l containing X_i (resp. Y_j), its properties are immediately derived from those of A. For example, if A is bounded, or compact, or convex, every $\hat{X}_i$ and every $\hat{Y}_j$ is respectively bounded, compact, convex.

5.5. PRIVATE OWNERSHIP ECONOMIES

The remainder of this chapter will study economies where the consumers own the resources and control the producers. Thus, the ith consumer receives the value of his *resources* ω_i (the ω_i are points of R^l satisfying $\sum_{i=1}^{m} \omega_i = \omega$, the total resources), and the *shares* $\theta_{i1}, \cdots, \theta_{ij}, \cdots, \theta_{in}$ of the profit of the 1st, $\cdots$, jth, $\cdots$, nth producer (the θ_{ij} are real numbers satisfying $\theta_{ij} \geqq 0$, and $\sum_{i=1}^{m} \theta_{ij} = 1$ for every j). The point ω_i specifies the *a priori given* quantities of commodities that are made available to him, or by him; the number θ_{ij} is interpreted as the fraction of the stock of the jth producer that he owns.

A complete description of a *private ownership economy* $\mathcal{E}$ therefore consists of:

For each consumer, his consumption set X_i, his preference preordering $\underset{\widetilde{i}}{\precsim}$, his resources $\omega_i \Big($satisfying $\sum_{i=1}^{m} \omega_i = \omega$, the total resources$\Big)$, and his shares $\theta_{i1}, \cdots, \theta_{ij}, \cdots, \theta_{in} \Big($satisfying $\theta_{ij} \geqq 0$, and $\sum_{i=1}^{m} \theta_{ij} = 1$ for every $j\Big)$.

For each producer, his production set Y_j.

Consider a private ownership economy $\mathcal{E}$. When the price system is p, the jth producer tries to maximize his profit on Y_j. Suppose that y_j does this; the profit $\pi_j(p) = p \cdot y_j$ is distributed to shareholders. Thus the wealth of the ith consumer is:

$$w_i = p \cdot \omega_i + \sum_{j=1}^{n} \theta_{ij} \pi_j(p).$$

This consumer tries to satisfy his preferences in X_i subject to his wealth constraint. Suppose that x_i does this. If the actions x_i, y_j satisfy the market equilibrium equality $x - y = \omega$, the economy is in equilibrium, i.e., every agent, given the price system and the actions of the other agents, has no incentive to choose a different action, and the state of the economy is a market equilibrium. Formally:

A private ownership economy $\mathcal{E}$ is defined by:

an economy $((X_i, \underset{\widetilde{i}}{\precsim}), (Y_j), \omega)$;

for each i, a point ω_i of R^l such that $\sum_{i=1}^{m} \omega_i = \omega$;

for each pair (i, j), a non-negative real number θ_{ij} such that $\sum_{i=1}^{m} \theta_{ij} = 1$ for every j.

An equilibrium of the private ownership economy $\mathcal{E}$ is an $(m + n + 1)$-tuple $((x_i^*), (y_j^*), p^*)$ of points of R^l such that:

(α) *x_i^* is a greatest element of $\{x_i \in X_i \mid p^* \cdot x_i \leqq p^* \cdot \omega_i + \sum_{j=1}^{n} \theta_{ij} p^* \cdot y_j^*\}$ for $\underset{\widetilde{i}}{\precsim}$, for every i,*

(β) *y_j^* maximizes profit relative to p^* on Y_j, for every j,*

(γ) *$x^* - y^* = \omega$.*

(α) expresses that, for the ith consumer, x_i^* is (see 4.9) an equilibrium consumption relative to (p^*, w^*) where $w_i^* = p^* \cdot \omega_i + \sum_{j=1}^{n} \theta_{ij} p^* \cdot y_j^*$;

(β) expresses that, for the jth producer, y_j^* is (see 3.4) an equilibrium production relative to p^*; (γ) expresses that the state $((x_i^*), (y_j^*))$ is a market equilibrium. Let t be a positive real number; $((x_i^*), (y_j^*), tp^*)$ is an equilibrium if and only if $((x_i^*), (y_j^*), p^*)$ is one; therefore all the price systems belonging to an open half-line with origin 0 are equivalent from the point of view of equilibrium.

The fundamental question arises at once: given a private ownership economy, does it have an equilibrium? An answer will be given in 5.7. A preliminary theorem will be proved in the next section.

5.6. Market Equilibrium

Consider a private ownership economy $\mathscr{E}$, and let C be the set of p in R^l for which all the sets $\eta_j(p)$, $\xi_i'(p)$ of this paragraph are defined (hence non-empty). When the price system is p in C, the jth producer chooses y_j in the set $\eta_j(p)$ of his productions optimal for that price system (see 3.4), and his profit is $\pi_j(p) = p \cdot y_j$. Hence the wealth distribution is the m-tuple $(p \cdot \omega_i + \sum_{j=1}^{n} \theta_{ij}\pi_j(p))$, and the ith consumer chooses x_i in the set

$$\xi_i\left(p, \left(p \cdot \omega_i + \sum_{j=1}^{n} \theta_{ij}\pi_j(p)\right)\right)$$

of his consumptions optimal for that price system and that wealth distribution (see 4.9). That set depends only on p and will be denoted $\xi_i'(p)$; the sum $\sum_{i=1}^{m} \xi_i'(p)$ will be denoted $\xi'(p)$. Since x_i is an arbitrary point of $\xi_i'(p)$ for every i and y_j is an arbitrary point of $\eta_j(p)$ for every j, the excess demand $z = x - y - \omega$ is an arbitrary point of the set

$$\zeta(p) = \xi'(p) - \eta(p) - \{\omega\},$$

a subset of $Z = X - Y - \{\omega\}$. Thus with each price system p in C is associated the non-empty set $\zeta(p)$ of excess demands compatible with the selection by every consumer of a consumption optimal for his wealth constraint and by every producer of a production optimal for that price system. The correspondence ζ from C to Z is called the *excess demand correspondence*. The equilibrium problem amounts to finding a p in C for which a corresponding excess demand is 0 and can thus be formulated: is there a p in C such that $0 \in \zeta(p)$?

Notice first that, if p is in C and t is a positive real number, $\eta_j(tp)$ is defined and equals $\eta_j(p)$ and $\xi_i'(tp)$ is defined and equals $\xi_i'(p)$; in other words, if all the prices of a price system p in C are multiplied by the same positive real number, the sets of optimal actions of the various agents are unchanged. Hence $tp \in C$ and $\zeta(tp) = \zeta(p)$. The first relation shows that C is a cone with vertex 0, but with the point 0 excluded if (and only if) some of the $\eta_j(p)$, $\xi_i'(p)$ are not defined when all prices are zero. This clearly occurs if and only if some consumer is insatiable.

Notice also that the actions x_i, y_j chosen by the agents for a price system p in C satisfy the wealth constraints

$$p \cdot x_i \leqq p \cdot \omega_i + \sum_{j=1}^{n} \theta_{ij} p \cdot y_j \quad \text{for every } i.$$

Summing over i, one obtains $\left(\text{recalling that } \sum_{i=1}^{m} \theta_{ij} = 1 \text{ for every } j\right)$:

$$p \cdot x \leqq p \cdot \omega + p \cdot y, \quad \text{i.e.,} \quad p \cdot z \leqq 0.$$

Therefore for any p in C one has "$p \cdot z \leqq 0$ for every z in $\zeta(p)$," *which will also be written* $p \cdot \zeta(p) \leqq 0$. When $p \neq 0$, this means that the set $\zeta(p)$ is below (with possibly points in) the hyperplane through 0 orthogonal to p.

A solution to the equilibrium problem will be given in the case where free disposal ((h) of 3.3) prevails (a more general case will be discussed in notes 2, 3). It is intuitive that the market equilibrium equality (γ) of 5.5 can then be replaced by the inequality $x^* - y^* \leqq \omega$: precise conditions under which this can be done will be given in the next section. The above inequality expresses that for every commodity the net demand is at most equal to the *a priori* given available quantity; it can also be written $z^* \leqq 0$. The equilibrium problem relative to this weaker condition amounts to finding a p in C for which a corresponding excess demand is $\leqq 0$, i.e., belongs to $-\Omega$, and can thus be formulated: is there a p in C such that $\zeta(p) \cap (-\Omega)$ is not empty?

Moreover, in the free disposal case, $\eta_j(p)$ is defined for every j only if $p \geqq 0$ (see end of 3.4); hence C is contained in Ω. If, in addition, the point 0 is excluded from C (i.e., if some consumer is insatiable), for every p in C one has $\sum_{h=1}^{l} p_h > 0$, hence $\zeta\left(\dfrac{1}{\sum\limits_{h=1}^{l} p_h} p\right) = \zeta(p)$; in the search for an equilibrium, every p in C can therefore be replaced by the point where the closed half-line $0, p$ intersects the set

$$P = \left\{ p \in \Omega \ \middle| \ \sum_{h=1}^{l} p_h = 1 \right\}.$$

The heuristic remarks of the two last paragraphs lead one to study the following problem. A correspondence ζ from P to Z is such that for every p in P one has $p \cdot \zeta(p) \leq 0$. What further conditions on ζ and Z insure that there is a p in P such that $\zeta(p) \cap (-\Omega) \neq \emptyset$? An answer is given by theorem (1), which is very intuitive at least for a 2-dimensional space R^l (in fig. 1, let p move from one end of P to the other).

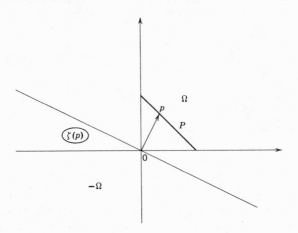

Fig. 1

(1) *Let Z be a compact subset of R^l. If ζ is an upper semicontinuous correspondence from P to Z such that, for every p in P, the set $\zeta(p)$ is (nonempty) convex and satisfies $p \cdot \zeta(p) \leq 0$, then there is a p in P such that $\zeta(p) \cap (-\Omega) \neq \emptyset$.*

Proof: P is easily seen to be non-empty, compact, and convex.

Z can be replaced by any compact subset Z' of R^l containing it; Z' is chosen to be convex. As P is non-empty, so, clearly, is Z, and hence Z'.

Given z in Z', let $\mu(z)$ be the set of p in P which maximize $p \cdot z$ on P. Since P is non-empty, compact, $\mu(z)$ is non-empty ((4') of 1.7) and the correspondence μ from Z' to P is upper semicontinuous on Z' (exactly as the supply correspondence η_j from R^l to Y_j was upper semicontinuous on R^l in 3.5). Since P is convex, $\mu(z)$ is also, for either (1) $z = 0$ and then $\mu(z)$ is P itself, or (2) $z \neq 0$ and then $\mu(z)$ is the intersection of P and the hyperplane $\{p \in R^l \mid p \cdot z = \text{Max } P \cdot z\}$.

Consider now the correspondence φ from $P \times Z'$ to itself defined by $\varphi(p, z) = \mu(z) \times \zeta(p)$. The set $P \times Z'$ (which is a subset of R^{2l}) is non-empty, compact, convex for P and Z' are. The correspondence φ is upper semicontinuous for μ and ζ are ((3) of 1.8). Finally, for all (p, z) in $P \times Z'$ the set $\varphi(p, z)$ is (non-empty) convex for $\mu(z)$ and $\zeta(p)$ are. Therefore all the conditions of Kakutani's theorem ((2) of 1.10.d) are satisfied, and φ has a fixed point (p^*, z^*). Thus $(p^*, z^*) \in \mu(z^*) \times \zeta(p^*)$, which is equivalent to:

(2) $p^* \in \mu(z^*)$ and $z^* \in \zeta(p^*)$.

The first relation in (2) implies that, for every p in P, one has $p \cdot z^* \leq p^* \cdot z^*$. The second implies that $p^* \cdot z^* \leq 0$. Hence, for every p in P, one has $p \cdot z^* \leq 0$. Letting k be one of the first l positive integers and taking the point p of P defined by $(p_k = 1, p_h = 0$ for $h \neq k)$, one obtains $z_k^* \leq 0$. Therefore $z^* \in -\Omega$. This, with $z^* \in \zeta(p^*)$, proves that p^* has the desired property.

The central idea of the proof consists, given an excess demand z, in choosing p in P so as to maximize $p \cdot z$. Let H be the set of commodities for which the component of z is the greatest. Maximizing $p \cdot z$ on P amounts to taking $p \geq 0$ such that $p_h = 0$ if $h \notin H$, and $\sum_{h \in H} p_h = 1$. This procedure is suggested by the remark made in 3.5: an increase in the price of a commodity increases, or leaves unchanged, the total supply of that commodity. This hints at a tendency for an increase in the price of a commodity to decrease the corresponding excess demand. It prompts one, when trying to reduce positive excess demands, to put the weight of the price system on those commodities for which the excess demand is the greatest.

5.7. EQUILIBRIUM

It is now possible to give an answer to the question raised at the end of 5.5.

(1)   *The private ownership economy* $\mathscr{E} = ((X_i, \underset{\widetilde{i}}{\prec}), (Y_j), (\omega_i), (\theta_{ij}))$ *has an equilibrium if:*

for every i   (a) X_i *is closed, convex, and has a lower bound for* $\leq$,

    (b.1)   *there is no satiation consumption in* X_i,

    (b.2)   *for every* x_i' *in* X_i, *the sets* $\{x_i \in X_i \mid x_i \underset{\widetilde{i}}{\succ} x_i'\}$ *and* $\{x_i \in X_i \mid x_i \underset{\widetilde{i}}{\prec} x_i'\}$ *are closed in* X_i,

(b.3)　if x_i^1 and x_i^2 are two points of X_i and if t is a real number
　　　　in $]0,1[$, then $x_i^2 \underset{i}{\succ} x_i^1$ implies $t x_i^2 + (1-t)x_i^1 \underset{i}{\succ} x_i^1$,

　(c)　there is x_i^0 in X_i such that $x_i^0 \ll \omega_i$;

for every j　(d.1)　$0 \in Y_j$;

　(d.2)　Y is closed and convex,

　(d.3)　$Y \cap (-Y) \subset \{0\}$,

　(d.4)　$Y \supset (-\Omega)$.

Proof: The theorem will be proved as an application of (1) of 5.6. Difficulties, however, arise from the fact that some of the sets Y_j may not be closed and convex, and some of the sets X_i, Y_j may be unbounded. In order to overcome them, the proof is organized as follows. Let $\overline{Y}_j$ denote the closed convex hull of Y_j, and let $\overline{\mathscr{E}}$ denote the private ownership economy obtained by substituting $\overline{Y}_j$ for Y_j in $\mathscr{E}$; in part 1, it is noticed that an $\mathscr{E}$-equilibrium is an $\overline{\mathscr{E}}$-equilibrium. In part 2, it is then shown that $\overline{\mathscr{E}}$-equilibrium actions x_i^*, y_j^* necessarily belong to well-chosen compact, convex subsets $\widehat{X}_i$, $\widehat{Y}_j$ of X_i, $\overline{Y}_j$. Denote now by a letter with the superior mark $\frown$, for example, $\widehat{\eta}_j$ the object defined from $\widehat{X}_i$, $\widehat{Y}_j$ exactly as the object denoted by that letter without the superior mark, for example η_j, was defined from X_i, Y_j. In particular, $\widehat{\mathscr{E}}$ will denote the private ownership economy obtained by substituting $\widehat{X}_i$ for X_i and $\widehat{Y}_j$ for Y_j in $\mathscr{E}$. It is easily checked that an $\overline{\mathscr{E}}$-equilibrium is an $\widehat{\mathscr{E}}$-equilibrium; hence an $\mathscr{E}$-equilibrium is an $\widehat{\mathscr{E}}$-equilibrium. Part 3 proves that an $\widehat{\mathscr{E}}$-equilibrium price system is necessarily the product of a vector of P by a positive number. One is thus led to study, instead of the initial $\widehat{\mathscr{E}}$-equilibrium problem, the $\widehat{\mathscr{E}}$-equilibrium problem where the price system is restricted to P. Part 4 establishes the upper semicontinuity on P of the correspondences $\widehat{\eta}_j$, $\widehat{\xi}_i'$. Part 5 then shows that all the conditions of (1) of 5.6 are satisfied for $\widehat{Z}$ and $\widehat{\zeta}$; hence there is p^* in P such that $\widehat{\zeta}(p^*)$ intersects $-\Omega$. The remaining task of parts 6, 7, 8 is to prove that p^* is actually an equilibrium price system for $\mathscr{E}$.

1. *An $\mathscr{E}$-equilibrium is an $\overline{\mathscr{E}}$-equilibrium.*

Let $\dot{Y}_j$ denote the convex hull of Y_j; thus $\overline{Y}_j$ denotes the closed convex hull of Y_j. The important fact that

(2)　　　　　　　　　　$\sum_j \overline{Y}_j = Y$

will be used in part 6; it is proved now. Clearly $Y_j \subset \bar{Y}_j$, hence $Y \subset \sum_j \bar{Y}_j$. On the other hand, according to (15) of 1.9, $\sum_j \dot{Y}_j = \dot{Y}$; hence, according to (1) of 1.9, $\sum_j \bar{Y}_j \subset \bar{Y}$. However, by (d.2), the last set is Y, and the result is established.

If $((x_i^*), (y_j^*), p^*)$ is an $\mathscr{E}$-equilibrium, it is also an $\bar{\mathscr{E}}$-equilibrium. To see this it suffices, according to the definition (α), (β), (γ) of 5.5, to check that, if y_j^* maximizes $p^* \cdot y_j$ on Y_j, it also maximizes $p^* \cdot y_j$ on $\bar{Y}_j$. But this is easily done for, if the closed, convex set $\{y_j \in R^l \mid p^* \cdot y_j \leqq p^* \cdot y_j^*\}$ contains Y_j, it also contains $\bar{Y}_j$.

2. *An $\bar{\mathscr{E}}$-equilibrium is an $\widehat{\mathscr{E}}$-equilibrium.*

Since "(d.3) and (d.4)" implies $Y \cap \Omega = \{0\}$, all the conditions of (2) of 5.4 are satisfied for $\bar{\mathscr{E}}$, and the set of its attainable states is bounded. Therefore, in $\bar{\mathscr{E}}$, the attainable consumption set of every consumer and the attainable production set of every producer (see end of 5.3) are bounded. Let then K be a closed cube of R^l with center 0 containing *in its interior* (the reason for this specification will appear in parts 7, 8) these $m + n$ sets. By definition:

$$\widehat{X}_i = X_i \cap K \quad \text{and} \quad \widehat{Y}_j = \bar{Y}_j \cap K.$$

It is clear that $\widehat{X}_i$ is compact, convex, satisfies (b.2), (b.3), and owns x_i^0 (indeed, on account of (c) and (d.4), x_i^0 is an attainable consumption for the ith consumer in $\bar{\mathscr{E}}$). It is also clear that $\widehat{Y}_j$ is compact, convex, and owns 0.

If $((x_i^*), (y_j^*), p^*)$ is an $\bar{\mathscr{E}}$-equilibrium, the state $((x_i^*), (y_j^*))$ is attainable for $\bar{\mathscr{E}}$, hence $x_i^* \in \widehat{X}_i$, which is a subset of X_i, and $y_j^* \in \widehat{Y}_j$, which is a subset of $\bar{Y}_j$, therefore $((x_i^*), (y_j^*), p^*)$ is an $\widehat{\mathscr{E}}$-equilibrium (see the definition (α), (β), (γ) of 5.5).

Summing up the conclusions of parts 1 and 2: an $\mathscr{E}$-equilibrium is an $\widehat{\mathscr{E}}$-equilibrium.

3. *An $\mathscr{E}$-equilibrium price system is > 0.*

Let p^* be an $\mathscr{E}$-equilibrium price system. Because of (b.1), $p^* \neq 0$; because of (d.4), $p^* \geqq 0$. Therefore $p^* > 0$, and the open half-line $0, p^*$ intersects the set P. Thus, in the search for an $\mathscr{E}$-equilibrium, the price system can, without any loss of generality, be restricted to be in P.

4. *Upper semicontinuity on P of $\widehat{\eta}_j$ and $\widehat{\xi}'_i$.*

Since $\widehat{Y}_j$ is compact, the supply correspondence $\widehat{\eta}_j$ from P to $\widehat{Y}_j$ is upper semicontinuous on P and the profit function $\widehat{\pi}_j$ from P to R is continuous on P ((3) of 3.5).

Since $x_i^0 \ll \omega_i$, for every p in P one has $p \cdot x_i^0 < p \cdot \omega_i$. Since $0 \in \widehat{Y}_j$, for every p in P one has $\widehat{\pi}_j(p) \geqq 0$. Hence, for every p in P, the inequality $p \cdot x_i^0 < p \cdot \omega_i + \sum_j \theta_{ij}\widehat{\pi}_j(p)$ holds, and the correspondence $\widehat{\gamma}_i$ is continuous at the point $(p, (p \cdot \omega_i + \sum_j \theta_{ij}\widehat{\pi}_j(p)))$ by (1) of 4.8. Since the function $\widehat{\pi}_j$ is continuous on P, so is the function which associates with each p in P the m-tuple of real numbers $(p \cdot \omega_i + \sum_j \theta_{ij}\widehat{\pi}_j(p))$. These remarks prove, with the help of (1) of 4.10 and (2) of 1.8, that the correspondence $\widehat{\xi}'_i$, defined at the beginning of 5.6, is upper semicontinuous on P.

5. *There is p^* in P and z in $-\Omega$ such that $z \in \widehat{\zeta}(p^*)$.*

The set $\widehat{Z} = \sum_i \widehat{X}_i - \sum_j \widehat{Y}_j - \{\omega\}$ is compact as a sum of compact sets. Since every $\widehat{\xi}'_i$ and every $\widehat{\eta}_j$ is upper semicontinuous on P, so is, by (4) of 1.9, the correspondence $\widehat{\zeta}$ defined at the beginning of 5.6. From the convexity of $\widehat{X}_i$, (b.2) and (b.3), follow that $\widehat{\xi}'_i(p)$ is convex for every p in P ("convexity of preferences and continuity of preferences" implies, by (1) of 4.7, "weak-convexity of preferences," and this, in turn, implies "convexity of $\widehat{\xi}'_i(p)$," see the discussion in 4.9). Similarly, from the convexity of $\widehat{Y}_j$ follows that $\widehat{\eta}_j(p)$ is convex for every p in P. Therefore $\widehat{\zeta}(p)$ is convex, as a sum of convex sets, for every p in P. Finally, exactly as in 5.6, $p \cdot \widehat{\zeta}(p) \leqq 0$ for every p in P. Thus all the conditions of (1) of 5.6 are satisfied, and the assertion of the title is proved.

6. *Definition of the $\mathscr{E}$-equilibrium actions x_i^* and y_j^*.*

Since $z \in \widehat{\zeta}(p^*)$, there is, for each i, a consumption x_i^* in $\widehat{\xi}'_i(p^*)$ and, for each j, a production y_j in $\widehat{\eta}_j(p^*)$ such that

$$(3) \qquad \sum_i x_i^* - \sum_j y_j - \omega = z.$$

Let y denote, as usual, the sum $\sum_j y_j$; as $y_j \in \overline{Y}_j$ for every j, the total production y belongs to Y by (2). The set Y is convex and closed, therefore "$y \in Y$ and $z \in -\Omega$" implies, by (2) of 3.3, "$y + z \in Y$." Hence there is, for each j, a production y_j^* in Y_j such that

(4) $$\sum_j y_j^* = y + z.$$

It will be proved that $((x_i^*), (y_j^*), p^*)$ is an equilibrium of $\mathscr{E}$. Notice first that "(3) and (4)" implies

(5) $$\sum_i x_i^* - \sum_j y_j^* - \omega = 0.$$

Therefore the state $((x_i^*), (y_j^*))$ is attainable for $\overline{\mathscr{E}}$, hence every x_i^* and every y_j^* is *in the interior* of the cube K.

7. *Properties of x_i^*.*

Define, then, w_i by

$$w_i = p^* \cdot \omega_i + \sum_j \theta_{ij} p^* \cdot y_j.$$

Since x_i^* is in $\widehat{\xi_i'}(p^*)$, the consumption x_i^* is, by definition of $\widehat{\xi_i'}$, a greatest element of the set $\widehat{\gamma_i}(p^*, w) = \{x_i \in \widehat{X_i} \mid p^* \cdot x_i \leq w_i\}$ for $\underset{i}{\precsim}$. Consequently:

(6) x_i^* is a greatest element of $\gamma_i(p^*, w) = \{x_i \in X_i \mid p^* \cdot x_i \leq w_i\}$ for $\underset{i}{\precsim}$.

If it were not so, there would be a consumption x_i' in $\gamma_i(p^*, w)$ such that $x_i' \underset{i}{\succ} x_i^*$. Let then $x_i(t)$ be the point $(1 - t)x_i^* + tx_i'$ where t is a real number in $]0, 1[$. For every such t, the point $x_i(t)$ would be in the set $\gamma_i(p^*, w)$ which is convex and, by (b.3), would satisfy the relation $x_i(t) \underset{i}{\succ} x_i^*$. Moreover, for t close enough to 0, the point $x_i(t)$ would be in the cube K (since x_i^* is in the interior of K), hence in $\widehat{\gamma_i}(p^*, w) = K \cap \gamma_i(p^*, w)$, and x_i^* would therefore not be a greatest element of $\widehat{\gamma_i}(p^*, w)$ for $\underset{i}{\precsim}$.

8. *Properties of y_j^*.*

From (6) and (2') of 4.9 follows that $p^* \cdot x_i^* = w_i$. Summing over i, one obtains, from the definition of w_i and (3) (and recalling that $\sum_i \theta_{ij} = 1$ for every j), $p^* \cdot z = 0$. Hence, from (4),

(7) $$p^* \cdot y^* = p^* \cdot y.$$

Since y_j is in $\widehat{\eta_j}(p^*)$, the production y_j maximizes profit (relative to p^*) on $\widehat{Y_j}$, for every j; therefore, by (1) of 3.4, y maximizes total profit on $\widehat{Y}$. From (7), so does y^*. And, by a new application of (1) of 3.4,

(8) y_j^* maximizes profit relative to p^* on $\widehat{Y_j}$, for every j.

In particular $p^* \cdot y_j^* = p^* \cdot y_j$, hence

$$w_i = p^* \cdot \omega_i + \sum_j \theta_{ij} p^* \cdot y_j^*.$$

This with (6) corresponds to (α) of the definition of $\mathscr{E}$-equilibrium given in 5.5, while (5) corresponds to (γ). As for

(β) y_j^* maximizes profit relative to p^* on Y_j, for every j,

it follows readily from (8): since y_j^* is interior to the cube K, an argument similar to that used for (6) proves that y_j^* maximizes profit relative to p^* on $\overline{Y_j}$ (hence on Y_j).

All the assumptions of theorem (1) have been discussed earlier with the exception of (c). The latter expresses that the ith consumer can obtain a possible consumption by disposing of a *positive* quantity of each commodity from his resources.

NOTES

1. The following are taken from K. J. Arrow and G. Debreu [1]: the concepts of attainable consumption and production sets and their boundedness properties (the term "attainable" is due to T. C. Koopmans [1]); the description of a private ownership economy; the central idea of the proof of (1) of 5.6; theorem (1) of 5.7 (modified according to the suggestion of H. Uzawa, [1] and private correspondence, to replace "every Y_j is convex" by "Y is convex").

Their article also contains historical remarks on the problem of existence of an equilibrium, and results where the inequality $\ll$ of assumption (c) of 5.7 is weakened to $<$ by means of the concept of always desired commodity.

2. Theorem (1) of 5.6 has, independently, been given by D. Gale [1] and H. Nikaido [1]. I thank A. Borel, P. Samuel, and A. Weil for the conversations I had with them on an early formulation of that result. An alternative proof will be found in H. W. Kuhn [2], a generalization to the case of non-free disposal in G. Debreu [5].

3. A brief account of the contributions of L. W. McKenzie [1], [2], [3] to the problem of equilibrium will now be presented.

The assumption of free disposal (d.4) in theorem (1) of 5.7 can be removed. Let *Int* **A** Y denote the interior of the asymptotic cone of Y. The theorem remains true if one replaces (d.4) by

(d'.4) $Y \cap \Omega \subset \{0\}$

and (c) by

(c') $(\{\omega_i\} + Int\ \mathbf{A}\ Y) \cap X_i \neq \emptyset;$

the proof requires only a few minor changes.

A still stronger result is obtained, without further modification of the proof, if the problem is treated in the smallest linear manifold L containing the set Z. Assume for a moment that (c') is replaced, in the set of assumptions of the last paragraph, by $(\{\omega_i\} +$

$\mathbf{A}Y) \cap X_i \neq \emptyset$. It is then easy to see that every set Y_j and every set $X_i - \{\omega_i\}$ is contained in L. Thus one can restrict oneself to the subspace L of the commodity space R^l (the component of the price system orthogonal to L being indeterminate). Therefore, denoting by $Int_L \mathbf{A}Y$ the interior of $\mathbf{A}Y$ *in L*, the existence theorem of 5.7 remains true, if one replaces (d.4) by

(d'.4) $Y \cap \Omega \subset \{0\}$

and (c) by

(c") $(\{\omega_i\} + Int_L \mathbf{A}Y) \cap X_i \neq \emptyset$.

It is possible to weaken further (c") by means of the concept of always desired commodity or by means of the concept, originating in D. Gale [2], of *irreducible* private ownership economy (L. W. McKenzie [2], [3]). In L. W. McKenzie [2] will also be found a study of the case where the preferences of a consumer depend on the actions of the other agents and on prices.

A model of production emphasizing international trade aspects is treated in L. W. McKenzie [1]. A similar model, without that particular emphasis, appears in R. Dorfman, P. A. Samuelson, and R. M. Solow [1], Chapter 13. Both are extensions of a model of A. Wald [1], [2], [3], a simple presentation of which is given in H. W. Kuhn [1].

4. Two important problems have not been studied in this chapter: the uniqueness and the stability of equilibrium (on this point see K. J. Arrow and L. Hurwicz [1], K. J. Arrow, H. D. Block, and L. Hurwicz [1], and their references).

CHAPTER 6 ✓

OPTIMUM

6.1. INTRODUCTION ✓

Given two attainable states of an economy, the second is considered to be at least as desirable as the first if every consumer desires his consumption in the second state at least as much as his consumption in the first. An optimum is thus defined as an attainable state such that, within the limitations imposed by the consumption sets, the production sets, and the total resources of the economy, one cannot satisfy better the preferences of any consumer without satisfying less well those of another.

The two main results of this chapter characterize an optimum by means of a new concept. Given a price system p, an attainable state is said to be an equilibrium relative to p if no consumer can satisfy his preferences better without increasing his expenditure and if no producer can increase his profit. In 6.3 it is shown, under certain weak assumptions, that, if an attainable state of an economy is an equilibrium relative to a price system, that state is an optimum. In 6.4 a converse assertion is proved under somewhat different assumptions: if an attainable state of an economy is an optimum, there is a price system relative to which that state is an equilibrium. To sum up briefly, an attainable state is an optimum if and only if there is a price system to which all the agents are adapted in the way described above. These two essential theorems of the theory of value thus explain the role of prices in an economy.

6.2. OPTIMUM AND EQUILIBRIUM RELATIVE TO A PRICE SYSTEM ✓

Consider the economy $E = ((X_i, \underset{\sim}{\preceq}), (Y_j), \omega)$. Given two attainable states of E, $((x_i), (y_j))$ and $((x_i'), (y_j'))$, the second is said to be at least as *desired* as the first, and one writes $((x_i), (y_j)), \underset{\sim}{\preceq} ((x_i'), (y_j'))$, if, for every i,

90

$x_i \underset{\sim}{\leq} x'_i$, i.e., if every consumer desires his consumption in the second state at least as much as his consumption in the first. It is easy to check that the relation $\underset{\sim}{\prec}$, defined on the set A of attainable states of E by this unanimity principle for consumers, is a preordering. It is clear that two attainable states of E may not be comparable, i.e., that the preordering $\underset{\sim}{\prec}$ may not be complete.

Let $((x_i), (y_j))$ and $((x'_i), (y'_j))$ be two attainable states of the economy E. According to the definition of 1.4.c, $((x_i), (y_j)) \prec ((x'_i), (y'_j))$ means: for every i, $x_i \underset{\sim}{\leq} x'_i$, and, for at least one i, $x_i \underset{i}{\prec} x'_i$. The second state is then said to be *preferred* to the first: every consumer desires his consumption in the second state at least as much as that in the first, and at least one consumer actually prefers his consumption in the second state to that in the first. Similarly, according to 1.4.c, $((x_i), (y_j)) \sim ((x'_i), (y'_j))$ means: for every i, $x_i \underset{i}{\sim} x'_i$. The two states are then said to be *indifferent*: for every consumer, his consumptions in the two states are indifferent.

An *optimum* of the economy E is now defined as an attainable state to which no attainable state is preferred. It is a maximal element of the set A for the preordering $\underset{\sim}{\prec}$. This can be paraphrased as follows: when an attainable state is not an optimum, it is possible, by suitable changes in productions and consumptions, to satisfy better the preferences of at least one consumer without satisfying less well those of any other; when an attainable state is an optimum, this is no longer possible, a better satisfaction of the preferences of a consumer necessarily occurs at the expense of the satisfaction of the preferences of another. Apart from the trivial case when they are indifferent, two optimums are not comparable.

The main definitions given above are gathered here:

A preordering $\underset{\sim}{\prec}$ is defined on the set A of attainable states of an economy E by $((x_i), (y_j)) \underset{\sim}{\prec} ((x'_i), (y'_j))$ if, for every i, $x_i \underset{i}{\leq} x'_i$. An optimum of E is a maximal element of A for $\underset{\sim}{\prec}$.

An intuitive representation of the set A preordered by $\underset{\sim}{\prec}$ in the space R^m ordered by $\leqq$ can be obtained in the case when, for every $i = 1, \cdots, m$, the consumption set X_i is connected and the preference preordering $\underset{i}{\prec}$ is continuous ((a) of 4.6). Then there is, for every i, a continuous utility function u_i from X_i to R ((1) of 4.6). Define the function u from A to R^m by associating with the attainable state $((x_i), (y_j))$ the m-tuple of real numbers $(u_i(x_i))$. It is clear that $((x_i), (y_j)) \underset{\sim}{\prec} ((x'_i), (y'_j))$ if and only if $u((x_i), (y_j)) \leqq u((x'_i), (y'_j))$. Comparing two attainable states for the preordering $\underset{\sim}{\prec}$ is therefore equivalent to comparing their images in R^m by the function u for the ordering $\leq$. In particular, an attainable state is preferred to another if and only if the image by u of the first $>$ the image by u of the second; two attainable states are indifferent if and only if their images by u are the same; an attainable state is an optimum if and only if its image by u is a maximal element for $\leq$ of the image $U = u(A)$ of A by u. Figure 1 illustrates the

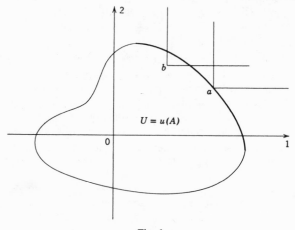

Fig. 1

above concepts in the case where there are two consumers in the economy E; it is drawn on the assumptions that the representation u of A in R^2 exists and that, moreover, the set $U = u(A)$ is compact (this last assumption will be discussed in the proof of (1)). A state represented by a, or by b, is preferred to a state represented by 0. A state is an optimum if and only if it is represented by a point in the heavy-lined part of the boundary of U. A state represented by a (which is an optimum) is *not* comparable to a state represented by b (which is *not* an optimum). Figure 1 emphasizes that an optimum is not necessarily unique, and that two optimums which are not indifferent are not comparable.

The preceding representation of A in R^m also gives an easy answer to the question: given an economy E, does it have an optimum?

(1)   *The economy $E = ((X_i, \underset{\widetilde{i}}{\prec}), (Y_j), \omega)$ has an optimum if: for every i,*

(a)   *X_i is closed, connected, and has a lower bound for $\leq$,*

92

(b) *for every x_i' in X_i, the sets $\{x_i \in X_i \mid x_i \underset{i}{\succ} x_i'\}$ and $\{x_i \in X_i \mid x_i \underset{i}{\precsim} x_i'\}$ are closed in X_i;*

(c) *Y is closed, convex, and satisfies $Y \cap \Omega = \{0\}$,*

(d) *$\omega \in X - Y$.*

Proof: According to (1) of 4.6, there is, for every i, a continuous utility function u_i. Hence the representation u of A in R^m exists, and is continuous. Finding an optimum of the economy E is then equivalent to finding a maximal element of the set $U = u(A)$ for the ordering $\leqq$ of R^m.

Consider the economy $E' = ((X_i, \underset{i}{\precsim}), Y, \omega)$ derived from the economy E by replacing the n production sets Y_j by their sum Y. Let A' be the set of attainable states of E'. Using the same utility functions u_i as above, one obtains the continuous representation u' of A' in R^m. It is easy to check that a point of R^m belongs to $u'(A')$ if and only if it belongs to $u(A)$, i.e., that $u'(A') = U$. But, according to (1) and (2) of 5.4, the set A' is closed and bounded. Therefore *the set U is compact* as the image of a compact set, A', by a continuous function, u' ((4) of 1.7). Moreover, by (d), *the set U is not empty.*

In order to have a maximal element of U for $\leqq$ it is clearly sufficient to maximize on U any continuous, increasing (see 1.4.k) function from R^m ordered by $\leqq$ to R.

An important characterization of an optimum will be given in the next two sections. To this end a new concept is introduced here. Given a price system p, a state $((x_i^*), (y_j^*))$ of an economy E is said to be an *equilibrium relative to p* if: (α) for the ith consumer, x_i^* is (see 4.9) an equilibrium consumption relative to p; (β) for the jth producer, y_j^* is (see 3.4) an equilibrium production relative to p; (γ) the state $((x_i^*), (y_j^*))$ is a market equilibrium. Formally:

A state $((x_i^*), (y_j^*))$ of E is an equilibrium relative to the price system p in R^l if:

(α) x_i^* *is a greatest element of $\{x_i \in X_i \mid p \cdot x_i \leqq p \cdot x_i^*\}$ for $\underset{i}{\precsim}$, for every i,*

(β) y_j^* *maximizes $p \cdot y_j$ on Y_j, for every j,*

(γ) $x^* - y^* = \omega$.

Clearly, if $((x_i^*), (y_j^*), p^*)$ is an equilibrium of a private ownership economy, the state $((x_i^*), (y_j^*))$ is an equilibrium relative to p^* for the corresponding economy. Conversely, let the state $((x_i^*), (y_j^*))$ be an equilibrium relative to p^* for an economy E; it is easy to check that $((x_i^*), (y_j^*), p^*)$ is an equilibrium of the private ownership economy obtained from E by giving to the ith consumer the resources $\omega_i = x_i^* - (1/m)y^*$ and the shares $\theta_{ij} = 1/m$. Summing up, the state $((x_i^*), (y_j^*))$ is an equilibrium relative to p^* for an economy E if and only if $((x_i^*), (y_j^*), p^*)$ is an equilibrium of a private ownership economy derived from E by specifying the resources and the shares of the consumers. The interest of the newly introduced concept is that it does not require such a specification.

It will be proved in the next two sections that, under proper assumptions on the economy E, and with an exception noted in 6.4, the concepts of optimum and of equilibrium relative to a price system are equivalent.

Consider an economy E and denote by $X_i^{x_i^*}$ the set $\{x_i \in X_i \mid x_i \underset{i}{\succsim} x_i^*\}$ of consumptions in X_i which the ith consumer desires at least as much as the consumption x_i^* in X_i. Given an m-tuple (x_i^*) of consumptions where $x_i^* \in X_i$ for every i, the set

$$(\delta) \qquad G = \sum_i X_i^{x_i^*} - \sum_j Y_j$$

is the set of total resources forming with $(X_i, \preceq)$ and (Y_j) an economy which can attain a state $((x_i), (y_j))$ such that $x_i \underset{i}{\succsim} x_i^*$ for every i. The proofs of theorems (1) of 6.3 and (1) of 6.4 consist essentially of a study of the relative position of the point ω (the actual total resources) and the set G (the set of total resources yielding an economy which can satisfy the preferences of consumers at least as well as some given m-tuple (x_i^*) of possible consumptions).

6.3. An Equilibrium Relative to a Price System is an Optimum ✓

(1) *Let E be an economy such that, for every i,*

(a) X_i *is convex,*

(b) *if x_i^1 and x_i^2 are two points of X_i and if t is a real number in $]0, 1[$, then $x_i^2 \underset{i}{\succ} x_i^1$ implies $t x_i^2 + (1 - t) x_i^1 \underset{i}{\succ} x_i^1$.* convexity

An equilibrium $((x_i^*), (y_j^*))$ relative to a price system p, where no x_i^* is a satiation consumption, is an optimum.

Proof: Consider the function from R^l to R defined by $a \to p \cdot a$. Since the conditions of (2) of 4.9 are satisfied, it follows from (α) of 6.2 that x_i^* minimizes $p \cdot a$ on $X_i^{x_i^*}$. Moreover, from (β) of 6.2, $-y_j^*$ minimizes $p \cdot a$ on $-Y_j$. Therefore, by (1) of 3.4, $\sum_i x_i^* - \sum_j y_j^*$, which is equal to ω, minimizes $p \cdot a$ on $G = \sum_i X_i^{x_i^*} - \sum_j Y_j$ (this shows, incidentally, that ω is in the boundary of G; see fig. 2).

Let, then, $((x_i), (y_j))$ be an attainable state such that $x_i \underset{\widetilde{i}}{\succ} x_i^*$ for every i. It will be proved that $x_i \underset{\widetilde{i}}{\sim} x_i^*$ for every i, and this will establish the theorem. Since $x - y = \omega$, the point $\sum_i x_i - \sum_j y_j$ minimizes $p \cdot a$ on G, and this implies, by (1) of 3.4, that x_i minimizes $p \cdot a$ on $X_i^{x_i}$ for every i. Therefore $p \cdot x_i \leqq p \cdot x_i^*$, and, by ($\alpha$) of 6.2, $x_i \underset{\widetilde{i}}{\preceq} x_i^*$, q.e.d.

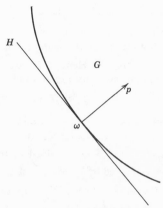

Fig. 2

6.4. An Optimum is an Equilibrium Relative to a Price System ✓

A deeper theorem will now be proved.

(1) *Let E be an economy such that: for every i,*

(a) *X_i is convex,*

(b.1) *for every x_i' in X_i, the sets $\{x_i \in X_i \mid x_i \underset{\widetilde{i}}{\succ} x_i'\}$ and $\{x_i \in X_i \mid x_i \underset{\widetilde{i}}{\preceq} x_i'\}$ are closed in X_i,*

(b.2) *if x_i^1 and x_i^2 are two points of X_i and if t is a real number in $]0, 1[$, then $x_i^2 \underset{i}{\succ} x_i^1$ implies $t x_i^2 + (1 - t) x_i^1 \underset{i}{\succ} x_i^1$;*

(c) *Y is convex.*

Given an optimum $((x_i^*), (y_j^*))$ where some $x_{i'}^*$ is not a satiation consumption, there is a price system p different from 0 such that:

(α) *x_i^* minimizes $p \cdot x_i$ on $\{x_i \in X_i \mid x_i \underset{\widetilde{i}}{\succ} x_i^*\}$, for every i,*

(β) *y_j^* maximizes $p \cdot y_j$ on Y_j, for every j.*

Proof: Let $\overset{\circ}{X}{}^{x^*_{i'}}_{i'}$ denote the set $\{x_{i'} \in X_{i'} \mid x_{i'} \underset{i'}{>} x^*_{i'}\}$ of consumptions in $X_{i'}$ which the i'th consumer prefers to the consumption $x^*_{i'}$ in $X_{i'}$. Consider now the set

$$\overset{\circ}{G} = \overset{\circ}{X}{}^{x^*_{i'}}_{i'} + \sum_{i \neq i'} X^{x^*_i}_i - \sum_j Y_j$$

of total resources forming with $(X_i, \underset{\widetilde{i}}{\leq})$ and (Y_j) an economy which can attain a state $((x_i), (y_j))$ such that $x_{i'} \underset{i'}{>} x^*_{i'}$ and $x_i \underset{\widetilde{i}}{>} x^*_i$ for $i \neq i'$. Since the state $((x^*_i), (y^*_j))$ is an optimum, ω *does not belong to* $\overset{\circ}{G}$. Moreover, it follows from (a), (b.1), and (b.2), by (1) of 4.7, that the sets $\overset{\circ}{X}{}^{x^*_{i'}}_{i'}$ and $X^{x^*_i}_i$ are convex. Hence $\overset{\circ}{G}$ *is convex* as a sum of convex sets. Thus, by Minkowski's theorem ((16) of 1.9.x), there is a hyperplane H through ω, bounding for $\overset{\circ}{G}$, i.e., there is p in R^l different from 0 such that $p \cdot a \geq p \cdot \omega$ for every a in $\overset{\circ}{G}$.

According to (2) of 4.7, if $x_{i'} \underset{i'}{\widetilde{\sim}} x^*_{i'}$, then $x_{i'}$ is adherent to $\overset{\circ}{X}{}^{x^*_{i'}}_{i'}$. In other words, the set $X^{x^*_{i'}}_{i'}$ is contained in the adherence of $\overset{\circ}{X}{}^{x^*_{i'}}_{i'}$. Therefore the set G defined by (δ) of 6.2 is contained in the sum of the adherences of the $m + n$ sets adding up to $\overset{\circ}{G}$. As this sum of adherences is, by (1) of 1.9.f, contained in the adherence of $\overset{\circ}{G}$, the set G is contained in the adherence of $\overset{\circ}{G}$, hence in the closed half-space above the hyperplane H. Since the point ω belongs to G, it minimizes $p \cdot a$ on G (thus ω is in the boundary of G; see fig. 2). It follows from $\omega = \sum_i x^*_i - \sum_j y^*_j$, by (1) of 3.4, that x^*_i minimizes $p \cdot a$ on $X^{x^*_i}_i$ for every i, and $-y^*_j$ minimizes $p \cdot a$ on $-Y_j$ for every j, q.e.d.

If the exceptional case where $p \cdot x^*_i$ is the smallest expenditure relative to p in the consumption set X_i does not occur, then (α) of 6.4 implies (α) of 6.2 by (1) of 4.9, and $((x^*_i), (y^*_j))$ is indeed an equilibrium relative to p.

NOTES

1. This chapter is based on K. J. Arrow [1] and G. Debreu [1], [4].

A bibliography on the problem of optimum will be found in the two survey articles A. Bergson [1], K. Boulding [1]. The most interesting treatments of this problem by the calculus have been given by O. Lange [1] and M. Allais [1], Chapter 4, Section E. The representation of the set of attainable states of an economy illustrated by fig. 1

is borrowed from M. Allais [1], Chapter 4, Section E, and P. A. Samuelson [1], Chapter 8, [2]. The set $\sum_i X_i^{*x_i}$ at the end of 6.2 is related to the concept of community indifference curve of T. Scitovsky [1].

2.   Theorems similar to (1) of 6.3 and (1) of 6.4 are proved when the commodity space is an arbitrary vector space over the reals in G. Debreu [4]. This provides, in particular, a solution of the problem of optimum when the dates form a sequence extending indefinitely in the future, a case studied by E. Malinvaud [1] with a different technique.

CHAPTER 7

UNCERTAINTY

7.1. INTRODUCTION

The analysis is extended in this chapter to the case where uncertain events determine the consumption sets, the production sets, and the resources of the economy. A contract for the transfer of a commodity now specifies, in addition to its physical properties, its location and its date, an event on the occurrence of which the transfer is conditional. This new definition of a commodity allows one to obtain a theory of uncertainty free from any probability concept and formally identical with the theory of certainty developed in the preceding chapters.

7.2. EVENTS

An economy whose activity extends over T elementary time-intervals, or dates, will be studied. It is assumed that the uncertainty of the environment during that period originates in the choice that Nature makes among a finite number of alternatives. These alternatives will be called *events at T* and indicated by an index e_T running from 1_T to k_T. Once e_T is given, atmospheric conditions, natural disasters, technical possibilities, ... are determined for the entire period.

At the beginning of date t, the agents of the economy have some information about the event at T which will obtain. This information can be formally presented as follows. The set of events at T is partitioned into non-empty subsets called *events at t* and indicated by an index e_t running from 1_t to k_t. At the beginning of date t, every agent knows to what event at t the event at T which will obtain belongs. At the beginning of date $t + 1$, further information is available, i.e., the partition which defines the events at $t + 1$ is derived by partitioning the events at t. The events at $t = 1, \cdots, T$ can be conveniently represented by the vertices of

98

a tree with the vertex 1_0 corresponding to the absence of information prevailing initially. In fig. 1 such an event tree is drawn for the particular case where $T = 3$.

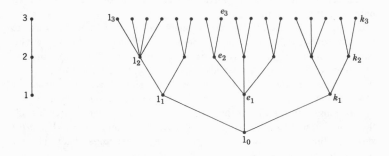

Fig. 1

7.3. COMMODITIES AND PRICES

Wheat with specified physical characteristics available at location s, at date t will play entirely different economic roles according to the event at t which obtains (in particular, according to precipitation during the growing season). One is thus led to define a *commodity* in this new context by its physical characteristics, its location, and its event (or vertex of the event tree; this vertex defining implicitly the date of the commodity). A contract for delivery of wheat between two agents takes, for example, the form: the first agent shall deliver to the second agent, who shall accept delivery, five thousand bushels of wheat of a specified type at location s, at event e_t. If e_t does not obtain, no delivery takes place. It was remarked in Chapter 2 that the definition of a certain commodity might require several dates (and several locations). Therefore the definition of an uncertain commodity may require here several events (and several locations). Summing up, the concept of uncertain commodity is derived from the concept of certain commodity by substituting the tree structure of events for the line structure of dates and replacing everywhere "date" by "event."

It is assumed that there is only a finite number l of commodities; these are indicated by an index h running from 1 to l. It is also assumed that the quantity of any one of them can be any real number. Given a sign convention for the inputs and the outputs of an *agent*, a complete plan of action, or more briefly an *action*, for him is represented by a point a of the *commodity space* R^l. The plan of action a made initially for the whole future specifies for each good and service the quantity that he will make available, or that will be made available to him, at each location, at each date, and at each event.

The *price* p_h of the hth commodity is a real number interpreted as the amount paid (in the sense of 2.1) initially by (resp. to) the agent who commits himself to accept (resp. to make) delivery of one unit of that commodity. Payment is irrevocably made although delivery does not take place if specified events do not obtain. An agent who buys a bushel of No. 2 Red Winter Wheat available in Chicago at date t *in any event* buys in fact as many commodities as there are events at t. The usual futures "price" thus corresponds to a *sum* of prices of uncertain commodities. The *price system* is the l-tuple $p = (p_1, \cdots, p_h, \cdots, p_l)$. The *value* of an action a relative to the price system p is the inner product $p \cdot a$.

7.4. PRODUCERS

An action y_j of the jth *producer* is called a *production* (inputs are negative and outputs positive). Let $y_j(e_T)$ denote the vector of the components of y_j associated with the unicursal path from the vertex 1_0 of the event tree to the vertex e_T, and let $Y_j[e_T]$ be the certain production set associated with the same path. The production y_j is possible if and only if $y_j(e_T)$ belongs to $Y_j[e_T]$ for every event e_T at T. The set of productions y_j possible for the jth producer is a subset of the commodity space R^l denoted Y_j and called the *production set* of the jth producer.

It is easy to interpret the assumptions of 3.3 on production sets in this new context, and to relate them to the corresponding assumptions in the case of certainty. For example, if $Y_j[e_T]$ is convex for every event e_T at T, then Y_j is clearly convex.

Given a price system p and a production y_j, the *profit* of the jth producer is $p \cdot y_j$. Considering the price system as a datum, the jth producer tries to maximize his profit in his production set. For this he needs neither an appraisal (conscious or unconscious) of the likelihoods of the various events, nor an attitude toward risk. His behavior amounts to maximizing the value of the stock outstanding of the jth corporation. In other words, the jth corporation announces a production plan y_j; as a result, its share has a determined value on the stock market; it chooses its plan so as to maximize the value of its share.

7.5. CONSUMERS

An action x_i of the ith *consumer* is called a *consumption* (inputs are positive and outputs negative). Exactly as for a producer, one defines the *consumption set* X_i of the ith consumer. It is assumed that the set X_i is completely preordered by the preferences $\underset{\widetilde{i}}{\preceq}$ of the ith consumer. This *preference preordering* reflects the tastes of the consumer for goods and services (including, in particular, their spatial and temporal specifications), his personal appraisal of the likelihoods of the various events, and his attitude toward risk.

The assumptions of 4.3 on consumption sets, and of 4.5–4.7 on preference preorderings are again easily interpreted in this context of uncertainty and related to the corresponding assumptions in the case of certainty. Most interesting are the three convexity assumptions on preferences of 4.7. Attention will be focused on:

(a) If $x_i^2 \underset{\widetilde{i}}{\succ} x_i^1$, then $tx_i^2 + (1 - t)x_i^1 \underset{\widetilde{i}}{\succ} x_i^1$,

which is the weakest (when preferences satisfy the continuity assumption (a) of 4.6). This axiom for uncertain consumptions implies an attitude of risk-aversion for the ith consumer. To see this, consider the case of one date and two events which are the outcomes *Head* and *Tail* of the tossing of a coin. Let b and c be two certain consumptions, and denote by (b, c) the uncertain consumption which associates b with event *Head* and c with event *Tail*, by (c, b) the uncertain consumption which makes the reverse association. Assume moreover that (b, b) is not indifferent to (c, c), i.e., that the certain consumptions b and c are not indifferent. If (b, c) is indifferent to (c, b), i.e., if the ith consumer appraises *Head* and *Tail* as being equally likely, (a) asserts that $((b + c)/2, (c + b)/2)$, i.e., the certainty of consuming $(b + c)/2$, is at least as desired as the uncertain consumption (b, c) or (c, b).

Given a price system p and his *wealth* w_i, the ith consumer tries to satisfy his preferences $\underset{\widetilde{i}}{\preceq}$ in the subset of X_i defined by the wealth constraint $p \cdot x_i \leqq w_i$.

7.6. EQUILIBRIUM

Finally the *total resources* are a given vector ω of R^l such that, for every event e_T at T, the vector $\omega(e_T)$ of the components of ω associated with the unicursal path from the vertex 1_0 of the event tree to the vertex e_T coincides with the certain total resources associated with that path. The formal description of an *economy* $E = ((X_i, \underset{\widetilde{i}}{\preceq}), (Y_j), \omega)$ is thus identical with that given in 5.3. In particular, an *attainable state* of E is an $(m + n)$-tuple $((x_i), (y_j))$ of actions such that

$$x_i \in X_i \text{ for every } i, y_j \in Y_j \text{ for every } j, \sum_{i=1}^{m} x_i - \sum_{j=1}^{n} y_j = \omega.$$

The equality expresses that the actions of the agents are compatible with the total resources, i.e., for every event e_T at T,

$$\sum_i x_i(e_T) - \sum_j y_j(e_T) = \omega(e_T).$$

A *private ownership economy* $\mathcal{E}$ is described by an economy $((X_i, \underset{\widetilde{\imath}}{\prec}),$ $(Y_j), \omega)$, the *resources* (ω_i) of the consumers and their *shares* (θ_{ij}). The ω_i are points of R^l satisfying $\sum_{i=1}^{m} \omega_i = \omega$, and the θ_{ij} are non-negative real numbers satisfying $\sum_{i=1}^{m} \theta_{ij} = 1$ for every j. Given a price system p and productions (y_j) for the n producers the wealth of the ith consumer is $w_i = p \cdot \omega_i + \sum_{j=1}^{n} \theta_{ij} p \cdot y_j$.

The formal identity of this theory of uncertainty with the theory of certainty developed earlier allows one to apply here all the results established in the preceding chapters. In particular, sufficient conditions for the existence of an equilibrium for the private ownership economy $\mathcal{E}$ are given by theorem (1) of 5.7.

7.7. OPTIMUM

In the same fashion, theorems (1) of 6.3 and (1) of 6.4 applied to the economy E yield sufficient conditions for an equilibrium relative to a price system to be an optimum, and for an optimum to be an equilibrium relative to a price system.

NOTES

1. This chapter is based on the mimeographed paper, "Une économie de l'incertain," written by the author at Electricité de France in the summer of 1953. The analysis of the theory of value under uncertainty in terms of choices of Nature originated in K. J. Arrow [2], where the risk-aversion implication of weak-convexity of preferences is established. The definition of the preference preordering in 7.5 has been suggested by the work of L. J. Savage [1].

A similar approach has been taken by E. Baudier [1]. A different attack has been tried by M. Allais [2].

2. The assumption that markets exist for all the uncertain commodities introduced in 7.3 is a natural extension of the usual assumption that markets exist for all the certain commodities of Chapter 2 (see in particular 2.6).

REFERENCES

Allais, M.
   [1] *A la recherche d'une discipline économique*, Paris, 1943. Reprinted as *Traité d'économie pure*, Paris, 1953.
   [2] "Généralisation des théories de l'équilibre économique général et du rendement social au cas du risque," *Econométrie*, Paris, Centre National de la Recherche Scientifique, 81–120, 1953.

Arrow, K. J.
   [1] "An Extension of the Basic Theorems of Classical Welfare Economics," *Proceedings of the Second Berkeley Symposium on Mathematical Statistics and Probability*, J. Neyman, ed., University of California Press, 507–532, 1951.
   [2] "Le rôle des valeurs boursières pour la répartition la meilleure des risques," *Econométrie*, Paris, Centre National de la Recherche Scientifique, 41–48, 1953.

Arrow, K. J., Block, H. D., and Hurwicz, L.
   [1] "On the Stability of the Competitive Equilibrium, II," *Econometrica*, 27, 1959.

Arrow, K. J., and Debreu, G.
   [1] "Existence of an Equilibrium for a Competitive Economy," *Econometrica*, 22, 265–290, 1954.

Arrow, K. J., and Hurwicz, L.
   [1] "On the Stability of the Competitive Equilibrium, I," *Econometrica*, 26, 522–552, 1958.

Baudier, E.
   [1] "L'introduction du temps dans la théorie de l'équilibre général," *Les cahiers économiques*, December 1954, 9–16.

Begle, E. G.
   [1] "A Fixed Point Theorem," *Annals of Mathematics*, 51, 544–550, 1950.

Berge, C.
   [1] *Espaces topologiques et fonctions multivoques*, Paris, Dunod, 1959.

Bergson, A.
   [1] "Socialist Economics," *A Survey of Contemporary Economics*, H. S. Ellis, ed., Philadelphia, Blakiston, 412–448, 1948.

Birkhoff, G.
   [1] *Lattice Theory*, American Mathematical Society Colloquium Publications, Vol. 25, 1940.

Block, H. D., Hurwicz, L., and Arrow, K. J.
   [1] See Arrow, Block, and Hurwicz.

Boulding, K.
   [1] "Welfare Economics," *A Survey of Contemporary Economics*, Vol. 2, B. F. Haley, ed., Homewood, Ill., Irwin, 1–38, 1952.

Bourbaki, N.
   [1] *Eléments de mathématique*, Paris, Hermann, 1939–

Cournot, A.

[1] *Recherches sur les principes mathématiques de la théorie des richesses*, Paris, Hachette, 1838. Translated as *Researches into the Mathematical Principles of the Theory of Wealth*, New York, Macmillan, 1929.

Debreu, G.

[1] "The Coefficient of Resource Utilization," *Econometrica, 19*, 273–292, 1951.

[2] "A Social Equilibrium Existence Theorem," *Proceedings of the National Academy of Sciences of the U.S.A., 38*, 886–893, 1952.

[3] "Representation of a Preference Ordering by a Numerical Function," *Decision Processes*, R. M. Thrall, C. H. Coombs, R. L. Davis, eds., New York, Wiley, 159–165, 1954.

[4] "Valuation Equilibrium and Pareto Optimum," *Proceedings of the National Academy of Sciences of the U.S.A., 40*, 588–592, 1954.

[5] "Market Equilibrium," *Proceedings of the National Academy of Sciences of the U.S.A., 42*, 876–878, 1956.

Debreu, G., and Arrow, K. J.

[1] See Arrow and Debreu.

Divisia, F.

[1] *Economique rationnelle*, Paris, Doin, 1928.

Dorfman, R., Samuelson, P. A., and Solow, R. M.

[1] *Linear Programming and Economic Analysis*, New York, McGraw-Hill, 1958.

Eilenberg, S.

[1] "Ordered Topological Spaces," *American Journal of Mathematics, 63*, 39–45, 1941.

Eilenberg, S., and Montgomery, D.

[1] "Fixed Point Theorems for Multi-Valued Transformations," *American Journal of Mathematics, 68*, 214–222, 1946.

Fenchel, W.

[1] *Convex Cones, Sets, and Functions*, mimeographed, Department of Mathematics, Princeton University, 1953.

deFinetti, B.

[1] "Sulle stratificazioni convesse," *Annali di matematica pura ed applicata*, (4) *30*, 173–183, 1949.

Gale, D.

[1] "The Law of Supply and Demand," *Mathematica Scandinavica, 3*, 155–169, 1955.

[2] "General Equilibrium for Linear Models," hectographed, the RAND Corporation, 1957.

Herstein, I. N., and Milnor, J.

[1] "An Axiomatic Approach to Measurable Utility," *Econometrica, 21*, 291–297, 1953.

Hicks, J. R.

[1] *Value and Capital*, Oxford, Clarendon Press, 1939.

Hotelling, H.

[1] "Edgeworth's Taxation Paradox and the Nature of Demand and Supply Functions," *Journal of Political Economy, 40*, 577–616, 1932.

Houthakker, H. S.

[1] "Compensated Changes in Quantities and Qualities Consumed," *Review of Economic Studies, 19*, 155–164, 1952.

REFERENCES

Hurwicz, L., and Arrow, K. J.
   [1] See Arrow and Hurwicz.
Hurwicz, L., Arrow, K. J., and Block, H. D.
   [1] See Arrow, Block, and Hurwicz.
Kakutani, S.
   [1] "A Generalization of Brouwer's Fixed Point Theorem," *Duke Mathematical Journal, 8*, 457–459, 1941.
Koopmans, T. C.
   [1] "Analysis of Production as an Efficient Combination of Activities," *Activity Analysis of Production and Allocation*, T. C. Koopmans, ed., New York, Wiley, 33–97, 1951.
   [2] *Three Essays on the State of Economic Science*, New York, McGraw-Hill, 1957.
Kuhn, H. W.
   [1] "On a Theorem of Wald," *Linear Inequalities and Related Systems*, H. W. Kuhn and A. W. Tucker, eds., Princeton University Press, 265–273, 1956.
   [2] "A Note on 'The Law of Supply and Demand,'" *Mathematica Scandinavica, 4*, 143–146, 1956.
Lange, O.
   [1] "The Foundations of Welfare Economics," *Econometrica, 10*, 215–228, 1942.
Lindahl, E.
   [1] "Prisbildningsproblemets uppläggning från kapitalteoretisk synpunkt," *Ekonomisk Tidskrift, 31*, 31–81, 1929. Translated as "The Place of Capital in the Theory of Price," *Studies in the Theory of Money and Capital*, E. Lindahl, New York, Rinehart, 269–350, 1939.
McKenzie, L. W.
   [1] "On Equilibrium in Graham's Model of World Trade and Other Competitive Systems," *Econometrica, 22*, 147–161, 1954.
   [2] "Competitive Equilibrium with Dependent Consumer Preferences," *Proceedings of the Second Symposium in Linear Programming*, H. A. Antosiewicz, ed., Washington, National Bureau of Standards, 277–294, 1955.
   [3] "On the Existence of General Equilibrium for a Competitive Market," *Econometrica, 27*, 1959.
Malinvaud, E.
   [1] "Capital Accumulation and Efficient Allocation of Resources," *Econometrica, 21*, 233–268, 1953.
Menger, K.
   [1] "Bemerkungen zu den Ertragsgesetzen," *Zeitschrift für Nationalökonomie, 7*, 25–56, 1936, and "Weitere Bemerkungen zu den Ertragsgesetzen," *ibid.*, 7, 388–397, 1936. Translated as "The Logic of the Laws of Return, a Study in Meta-economics," *Economic Activity Analysis*, O. Morgenstern, ed., New York, Wiley, 419–482, 1954.
Milnor, J., and Herstein, I. N.
   [1] See Herstein and Milnor.
Montgomery, D., and Eilenberg, S.
   [1] See Eilenberg and Montgomery.
Morgenstern, O. and von Neumann, J.
   [1] See von Neumann and Morgenstern.

105

Nash, J. F.
[1] "Equilibrium Points in N-Person Games," *Proceedings of the National Academy of Sciences of the U.S.A., 36*, 48–49, 1950.

von Neumann, J.
[1] "Zur Theorie der Gesellschaftsspiele," *Mathematische Annalen, 100*, 295–320, 1928.
[2] "Über ein ökonomisches Gleichungssystem und eine Verallgemeinerung des Brouwerschen Fixpunktsatzes," *Ergebnisse eines mathematischen Kolloquiums*, No. 8, 73–83, 1937. Translated as "A Model of General Economic Equilibrium," *Review of Economic Studies, 13*, 1–9, 1945.

von Neumann, J., and Morgenstern, O.
[1] *Theory of Games and Economic Behavior*, Princeton University Press, 1944.

Nikaido, H.
[1] "On the Classical Multilateral Exchange Problem," *Metroeconomica, 8*, 135–145, 1956.

Pareto, V.
[1] *Cours d'économie politique*, Lausanne, Rouge, 1896–1897.
[2] *Manuale di economia politica*, Milano, Società Editrice Libraria, 1906. Translated and revised as *Manuel d'économie politique*, Paris, Giard, 1909.
[3] *Trattato di sociologia generale*, Firenze, Barbèra, 1916. Translated as *The Mind and Society*, New York, Harcourt, Brace, 1935.
[4] "Anwendungen der Mathematik auf Nationalökonomie," *Encyklopädie der mathematischen Wissenschaften*, Leipzig, Teubner, tome 1, volume 2, 1094–1120, 1902. Translated and revised as "Economie mathématique," *Encyclopédie des sciences mathématiques*, Paris, Gauthier-Villars, tome 1, volume 4, 591–640, 1911. The latter translated as "Mathematical Economics," *International Economic Papers*, No. 5, New York, Macmillan, 58–102, 1955.

Patinkin, D.
[1] *Money, Interest, and Prices*, Evanston, Ill., Row, Peterson, 1956.

Roy, R.
[1] *De l'utilité*, Paris, Hermann, 1942.

Samuelson, P. A.
[1] *Foundations of Economic Analysis*, Cambridge, Harvard University Press, 1947.
[2] "Evaluation of Real National Income," *Oxford Economic Papers*, (New Series) 2, 1–29, 1950.

Samuelson, P. A., Solow, R. M., and Dorfman, R.
[1] See Dorfman, Samuelson, and Solow.

Savage, L. J.
[1] *The Foundations of Statistics*, New York, Wiley, 1954.

Scitovsky, T.
[1] "A Reconsideration of the Theory of Tariffs," *Review of Economic Studies, 9*, 89–110, 1942.

Solow, R. M., Dorfman, R., and Samuelson, P. A.
[1] See Dorfman, Samuelson, and Solow.

Stigler, G. J.
[1] "The Development of Utility Theory," *Journal of Political Economy, 58*, 307–327, 373–396, 1950.

REFERENCES

Tintner, G.
  [1] "The Maximization of Utility over Time," *Econometrica*, 6, 154–158, 1938.
  [2] "The Theoretical Derivation of Dynamic Demand Curves," *Econometrica*, 6, 375–380, 1938.

Uzawa, H.
  [1] "Note on the Existence of an Equilibrium for a Competitive Economy," mimeographed, Department of Economics, Stanford University, 1956.

Wald, A.
  [1] "Über die eindeutige positive Lösbarkeit der neuen Produktionsgleichungen," *Ergebnisse eines mathematischen Kolloquiums*, No. 6, 12–20, 1935.
  [2] "Über die Produktionsgleichungen der ökonomischen Wertlehre," *Ergebnisse eines mathematischen Kolloquiums*, No. 7, 1–6, 1936.
  [3] "Über einige Gleichungssysteme der mathematischen Ökonomie," *Zeitschrift für Nationalökonomie*, 7, 637–670, 1936. Translated as "On Some Systems of Equations of Mathematical Economics," *Econometrica*, 19, 368–403, 1951.

Walras, L.
  [1] *Eléments d'économie politique pure*, Lausanne, Corbaz, 1874–1877. Translated as *Elements of Pure Economics*, Homewood, Ill., Irwin, 1954.

Wold, H.
  [1] "A Synthesis of Pure Demand Analysis," *Skandinavisk Aktuarietidskrift*, 26, 85–118, 220–263, 1943; 27, 69–120, 1944.

INDEX

Symbols

$\{\cdots\}$ 2
$\{\cdots \mid \cdots\}$ 3
$=, \neq$ 3
$\epsilon, \notin$ 3
$\subset$ 3
$\cup, \cap, \bigcup, \bigcap$ 4
N 2
J, Q 11
R 10
R^m 12
Ω 26
$\emptyset$ 3
0, 1 (in R) 10
0 (in R^m) 12
$(x, y), (x_1, \cdots, x_m), (x_i)$ 4
$(x^1, \cdots, x^q, \cdots), (x^q)$ 7
$S \times T, \prod_{i=1}^{m} S_i$ 4
$f^{-1}(Y)$ 5
$x \rightarrow f(x)$ 5
$x^q \rightarrow x^0$ 11, 12
c_S, c 4
A 22
$\lesssim, \gtrsim$ 7
$\sim, <, >$ 8

$\ll$ 9
$\leqq, \geqq, <, >$ (numbers) 10, (vectors) 26
$\ll, \leq$ 26
$[a, b], [a, b[, [a, \rightarrow[,]a, b[,]a, b],]\leftarrow, b]$ 9
$[x, y]$ 21
$x + y$ (numbers) 10, (vectors) 19, (sets) 20
$x \cdot y$ (numbers) 10, (vectors) 24
xy (numbers) 10, (number and vector) 20
$-x, x - y$ (numbers) 10, (vectors) 20, (sets) 20
$1/x, x/y$ 10
x^n 10
$x^{1/n}$ 11
$|x|$ (number) 10, (vector) 14
$\sum_{j=1}^{n} x_j$ (numbers) 10, (vectors) 20, (sets) 20
sign 10
Max, Min 10
Sup, Inf 10, 11
$\overline{X}$ 12
$\dot{S}$ 24
C° 25

Names and Terms

Above a hyperplane, 24
Absolute value, 10
Accumulation factor, 34
Action, 32, 35, 100
Addition for numbers, 10
Additivity for a production set, 41
Adherence, 12, 13
Adherent point, 12
Agent, 32, 35, 99
Allais, M., ix, 96, 97, 102
Arrow, K. J., ix, 35, 72, 73, 88, 89, 96, 102
Associative operation, 6
Asymptotic cone, 22
Attainable consumption, 76
Attainable consumption set, 76
Attainable production, 76
Attainable production set, 76
Attainable state, 76, 102
Average, weighted, 21

Baudier, E., 102
Begle, E. G., 27
Belong to a set, 3
Below a hyperplane, 24
Berge, C., 27
Bergson, A., 96
Binary operation, 6
Binary relation, 7
Birkhoff, G., 27
Block, H. D., 89
Bolzano, B., 17
Borel, A., 88
Boulding, K., 96
Bound, greatest lower, 9
  least upper, 9
  lower, 9
  upper, 9
Boundary, 14
Bounded set, 14
Boundedness for a consumption set, lower, 53
Bounding hyperplane, 24
Bourbaki, N., 27
Brouwer, L. E. J., 26

Cantor, G., 27
Center of a cube, 14
Class, 2
Closed convex hull, 24
Closed half-line, 21
Closed half-space, 24
Closed segment, 21
Closed set, 13
Closure, 12
Collection, 2
Commodity, 32, 35, 99
Commodity space, 32, 35, 100
Commutative operation, 6
Compact set, 15
Complement, 3, 4
Complete preordering, 8
Component of a tuple, 4
Cone, 21
Connected set, 15
Connectedness for a consumption set, 53
Constant function, 5
Constant returns to scale, 41
Consumer, 50, 52, 101
Consumption, 51, 52, 101
Consumption set, 51, 52, 101
Contain a set, 3
Continuity, for a consumption set, 52
  for a preference preordering, 56
  for a production set, 39
Continuous correspondence, 18
Continuous function, 15
Converge, 11, 12
Convergent sequence, 11, 12
Convex hull, 24
  closed, 24
Convex polyhedral cone, 23
Convex set, 23
Convexity, for a consumption set, 53
  for a preference preordering, 60
  for a production set, 41
Coordinate of a tuple, 4
Coordinate subspace, 12
Correspondence, 6
Countable set, 7
Cournot, A., vii

Cowles, A., ix
Cube, 14

Darmois, G., ix
Date, 29
Debreu, G., ix, 27, 72, 73, 88, 96, 97
Dedekind, R., 27
Degenerate segment, 21
Demand, 51, 52
Demand correspondence, 66, 67
Dense set, 13
Desired as, at least as, 54, 90
  at most as, 54, 90
Difference for numbers, 10
Different elements, 3
Dimension of a space, 12
m-Dimensional space, 12
Discount factor, 34
Discount rate, 34
Discounted price, 34
Disjoint sets, 4
  pairwise, 4
Distributive operation, 6
Divisia, F., ix
Division for numbers, 10
Dorfman, R., ix, 89

Economy, 75, 101
Edge of a cube, 14
Eilenberg, S., 27, 73
Element, 2
Empty set, 3
Equal elements, 3
Equilibrium, market, 76
  of a private ownership economy, 79,
    102
  relative to a price system, 93
Equilibrium consumption, relative to a
    price system, 66
  relative to a price-wealth pair, 65
Equilibrium production relative to a
    price system, 43
Euclidean space, 12
Events, 98
Excess demand, 75, 76
Excess demand correspondence, 80
Exchange rate, 34
Expenditure, 62

Extension of a function, 5
Exterior, 14
External economies and diseconomies, 49
Extremity of an interval, 11

Fenchel, W., 27, 73
Finetti, B. de, 73
Finite number, 10
Fixed point, 26
Free commodity, 33
Free disposal, 42
Free entry, 41
Free production, impossibility of, 40
Function, 5

Gale, D., 88, 89
Good, 29
Graph, of a correspondence, 6
  of a function, 5
Greatest element, 8
Greatest lower bound, 9

Half-line, closed, 21
  open, 21
Half-space, closed, 24
Herstein, I. N., 27, 73
Hicks, J. R., 35
Hotelling, H., 73
Houthakker, H. S., 73
Hurwicz, L., 89
Hyperplane, 24

Image by a function, 5
  inverse, 5
Impossibility of free production, 40
Inaction, possibility of, 40
Increasing function, 9
Increasing returns to scale, 41
Indifference class, 54, 55
Indifference relation, 54
Indifferent, 54, 91
Indirect utility, 67
Inequality, 10
Infimum, 11
Inner product, 24
Input, 30
Insatiability, 55
Integers, 11

Interest rate, 34
Interior, 14
Intersection, 4
Interval, 9
Inverse image by a function, 5
Inverse of a number, 10
Irreversibility for a production set, 40

Kakutani, S., vii, 2, 26, 27, 83
Koopmans, T. C., viii, ix, 35, 49, 88
Kuhn, H. W., 88, 89

Lange, O., 96
Lavaill, H., 72
Least element, 8
Least upper bound, 9
Length of an interval, 11
Leontief, W., ix
Less than, 10
Lexicographic ordering, 72
Life span, 52
Limit, 11, 12
Lindahl, E., 35
Linear manifold, 24
Location, 29
Lower bound, 9
  greatest, 9
Lower boundedness for a consumption
  set, 53
Lower semi-continuous correspondence,
  17, 18

McKenzie, L. W., ix, 88, 89
Malinvaud, E., 97
Manifold, linear, 24
Market equilibrium, 76
Marschak, J., ix
Massé, P., ix
Maximal element, 8
Maximizer of a function, 16
Maximum, of a function, 16
  of a set, 10
Menger, K., 49
Milnor, J., 27, 73
Minimal element, 8
Minimizer of a function, 16
Minimum, of a function, 16
  of a set, 10

Minkowski, H., 2, 25, 96
Montgomery, D., 27
More than, 10
Morgenstern, O., viii
Multiplication for numbers, 10
Multi-valued function, 27

Nash, J., vii
Nation, 35
Negative, of a number, 10
  of a vector, 20
Negative number, 10
Net demand, 75, 76
Neumann, J. von, vii, viii
Nikaido, H., 88
Non-decreasing returns to scale, 40
Non-increasing returns to scale, 40
Non-negative orthant, 26
Norm, 14
Normal for a hyperplane, 24
Noxious commodity, 33
Number, 10

One-to-one correspondence, 5
Onto, function, 5
Open half-line, 21
Operation, binary, 6
Optimum of an economy, 91, 102
Ordering, 7
  of R^m, 26
Origin, of a half-line, 21
  of an interval, 11
  of R^m, 12
Orthant, non-negative, 26
Orthogonal, 24
Output, 30
Own an element, 3

Pair, 4
Pairwise disjoint sets, 4
Pareto, V., vii
Partial preordering, 8
Partition of a set, 4
Patinkin, D., 36
Point, 11, 12
Polar of a cone, 25
Polyhedral cone, convex, 23
Positive number, 10

Positively semi-independent cones, 22
Possibility of inaction, 40
Power of a number, 10
Preference preordering, 54, 55, 101
Preferred, 54, 91
Preordering, 7
   on a product, 9
Price, 32, 100
   at a location, at a date, 33
Price system, 33, 35, 100
   at a location, at a date, 33
Price-wealth pair, 62
Private ownership economy, 79, 102
Producer, 37, 39, 100
Product, inner, 24
   of a vector and a number, 20
   of numbers, 10
   of sets, 4
Production, 38, 39, 100
Production set, 38, 39, 100
Profit, 43, 100
Profit function, 44
Projection, 6
Property of an element, 3

Quasi-concave function, 73
Quasi-ordering, 7
Quotient for numbers, 10

Radner, R., ix
Rank of an element, 7
Rational number, 11
Real number, 10
Reflexivity, 7
Relation, binary, 7
Representation, 9
Resources of a consumer, 78, 102
Root of a number, 11
Roy, R., ix, 73

Samuel, P., 88
Samuelson, P. A., ix, 49, 89, 97
Satiation, 54, 55
Savage, L. J., 102
Scarce commodity, 33
Scitovsky, T., 97
Segment, closed, 21
Sequence, 7

Service, 30
Set, 2
Shares of a consumer, 78, 102
Sign of a number, 10
Solow, R. M., ix, 89
State of an economy, 75
Stigler, G. J., 72
Straight line, 21
Strong-convexity for a preference preordering, 61
Subset, 3
Subtraction for numbers, 10
Sum, of numbers, 10
   of sets, 20
   of vectors, 19
Supply, 38, 39
Supply correspondence, 44
Supremum, 10

Tend, 11, 12
Thick indifference class, 59
Through a point, 24
Tintner, G., 35
Tobin, J., ix
Total consumption, 52
Total consumption set, 52
Total demand, 52
Total demand correspondence, 67
Total production, 38, 39
Total production set, 38, 39
Total profit, 43
Total profit function, 44
Total resources, 74, 75, 101
Total supply, 38, 39
Total supply correspondence, 44
Transform, 5
Transformation, 5
Transitivity, 7
Translation, 20
Tuple, 4

Unbounded set, 14
Union, 4
Upper bound, 9
   least, 9
Upper semi-continuous correspondence, 17, 18

Utility, 56
 indirect, 67
Uzawa, H., 88

Value, of a function, 5
 of an action, 33, 35, 100
Variable, 5
Vector, 20
Vertex of a cone, 21
Vickrey, W., 72

Wald, A., vii, 89

Walras, L., vii
Weak-convexity for a preference pre-
 ordering, 59
Wealth, 62, 101
Wealth constraint, 62
Wealth distribution, 62
Wealth hyperplane, 62
Weierstrass, K., 16
Weight for an average, 21
Weighted average, 21
Weil, A., 88
Wold, H., 73

COWLES FOUNDATION MONOGRAPHS

1. Charles F. Roos, *Dynamic Economics* (out of print)
2. Charles F. Roos, *NRA Economic Planning* (out of print)
3. Alfred Cowles and Associates, *Common-Stock Indexes* (2d edition)
4. Dickson H. Leavens, *Silver Money* (out of print)
5. Gerhard Tintner, *The Variate Difference Method* (out of print)
6. Harold T. Davis, *The Analysis of Economic Time Series* (out of print)
7. Jacob L. Mosak, *General-Equilibrium Theory in International Trade* (out of print)
8. Oscar Lange, *Price Flexibility and Employment*
9. George Katona, *Price Control and Business* (out of print)
10. Tjalling C. Koopmans, ed., *Statistical Inference in Dynamic Economic Models* (out of print)
11. Lawrence R. Klein, *Economic Fluctuations in the United States, 1921–1941* (out of print)
12. Kenneth J. Arrow, *Social Choice and Individual Values* (2d edition)
13. Tjalling C. Koopmans, ed., *Activity Analysis of Production and Allocation*
14. William C. Hood and Tjalling C. Koopmans, eds., *Studies in Econometric Method*
15. Clifford Hildreth and F. G. Jarrett, *A Statistical Study of Livestock Production and Marketing*
16. Harry M. Markowitz, *Portfolio Selection: Efficient Diversification of Investments*
17. Gerald Debreu, *Theory of Value: An Axiomatic Analysis of Economic Equilibrium*
18. Alan S. Manne and Harry M. Markowitz, eds., *Studies in Process Analysis: Economy-Wide Production Capabilities* (out of print)
19. Donald D. Hester and James Tobin, eds., *Risk Aversion and Portfolio Choice*
20. Donald D. Hester and James Tobin, eds., *Studies of Portfolio Behavior*
21. Donald D. Hester and James Tobin, eds., *Financial Markets and Economic Activity*
22. Jacob Marschak and Roy Radner, *Economic Theory of Teams*
23. Thomas J. Rothenberg, *Efficient Estimation with A Priori Information*
24. Herbert Scarf, *The Computation of Economic Equilibria*
25. Donald D. Hester and James L. Pierce, *Bank Management and Portfolio Behavior*

Orders for Monograph 8 should be sent to Principia Press of Trinity University, 715 Stadium Drive, San Antonio, Texas.

Orders for Monograph 3 should be sent to Cowles Foundation, Box 2125 Yale Station, New Haven, Conn. 06520.

Orders for Monographs 12, 13, 14, 16, 17, 21, 22, 23, 24, and 25 should be sent to Yale University Press, 92A Yale Station, New Haven, Conn. 06520.

Orders for Monographs 15, 19, and 20 should be sent to John Wiley & Sons, Inc., 605 Third Avenue, New York, N.Y. 10016.